Introduct

C000285757

For those of you who are unfamilia
it is centred on the old village of Ta
Aberystwyth. The village, which has two
in the foothills of the Cambrian Mountain
Bay and 8 miles from the summit of Pumlumon. Walking in this area is
a peaceful occupation – there are none of the crowds of Snowdonia. The
walks described are to the west of the Pumlumon ridge, bounded on the
north by the Afon Dyfi and to the south by the Afon Rheidol. The terrain
in this part of Wales is formed from a semi-circular plateau spreading
out from the base of the Pumlumon ridge at about 1600 feet. The edges
of the plateau have been eroded by ice and water into deep and often
isolated valleys, which form the dominant features of the walks.

As well as farming, the other occupations of industrial Talybont
were mining and weaving. The common feature of both was the need for
power. Both industries employed the same source of energy – waterpow-
er. The water wheels drove the winding gear and crushers at the mines
and powered the weaving frames and spinning jennies of the mills.

Although streams and rivers abound in the locality, they were not
always in the right place and could run dry in summer, so reservoirs
were constructed – most of the lakes boast a dam, showing them to be
either an enlarged natural pond or to have been created from scratch.
To conduct the water to the right place, channels called leats were built,
running at a very shallow gradient from the source to the wheel. The
largest, Taylor's Leat, was built about 1850, ran for 19 miles and supplied up to 50 wheels.

As very few mines were worked in the twentieth century, nature
has had over 100 years to soften their impact and most are now far from
being an eyesore. Many still have open adits (levels) and shafts, *and I
must emphasise that all are dangerous and should not be entered.*

The word 'forest' should not be taken too literally – it can mean
trees between one and one-hundred feet tall or even clear-cut woodland.
Logging operations may temporarily close some of the forest sections of
these walks but it is usually possible to find a detour.

Each walk has a detailed map and description which enables the
route to be followed without difficulty, but be aware that changes in
detail can occur at any time. The location of each walk is shown on the
back cover and a summary of their key features is also given. This also
includes an estimated walking time, but allow more to enjoy the scen-
ery. And please *always* observe the country code.

Enjoy your walking!

POOH-STICKS BRIDGE

DESCRIPTION A short walk of just under 2 miles, ideal for youngsters. It has a high point of only 325 feet, but still gives good views of the Dyfi estuary. Climb by a lane and grassy path, go down a forest path to the bridge and return by a lane. There is scope for a small adventure from the bridge, which adds ¼ mile. Allow 1 to 1½ hours for this route.

START Dyfi Furnace car park [SN 685952]

DIRECTIONS From Aberystwyth, turn west off the A487 in Furnace, just before the river bridge, into the very handy car park.

I From the car park, cross the main road and turn left over the bridge by Dyfi Furnace, admiring the wheel and waterfall. About 100 yards past the bridge, take the lane on the right, beyond the houses. The lane rises round to the right and soon levels out in trees. Just before the cattle grid sign the sound of water through the trees, beyond the broken wall on the right, lets you know you are now above the waterfall and wheel. Cross the cattle grid and climb over the stile on the left. Take the footpath up to the right, through the bracken, to meet the road again in about 75 yards. Bear left on the road and round the hairpin bend by the seat, *taking the opportunity for fine views of the Dyfi estuary.* Keep to the road and bear left about 200 yards beyond the first seat.

2 After 500 yards and a slight descent, take the smaller lane, at the footpath sign on the right, down to a cottage. Just before the cottage, go right through the wicket gate and down the path through the trees to Pooh-sticks Bridge. Collect you sticks and play the game! Just before the bridge is a stile into the field on the left. Over the stile, cross the little footbridge and head up the field in line with the power pole to the track under the trees. Follow the track to the right, up the valley under the trees, for about 200 yards, to cross the fence at a stile and continue up stream for 75 yards or so until the path disappears and the right of way stops. The length of this track is littered with fallen trees but the river in its little gorge below and the peaceful atmosphere at the end of the track make the detour worthwhile. Back at Pooh-sticks Bridge, cross and climb the path to the right, to meet the tarmac lane, which you follow back to Furnace, where you turn right to return to the start.

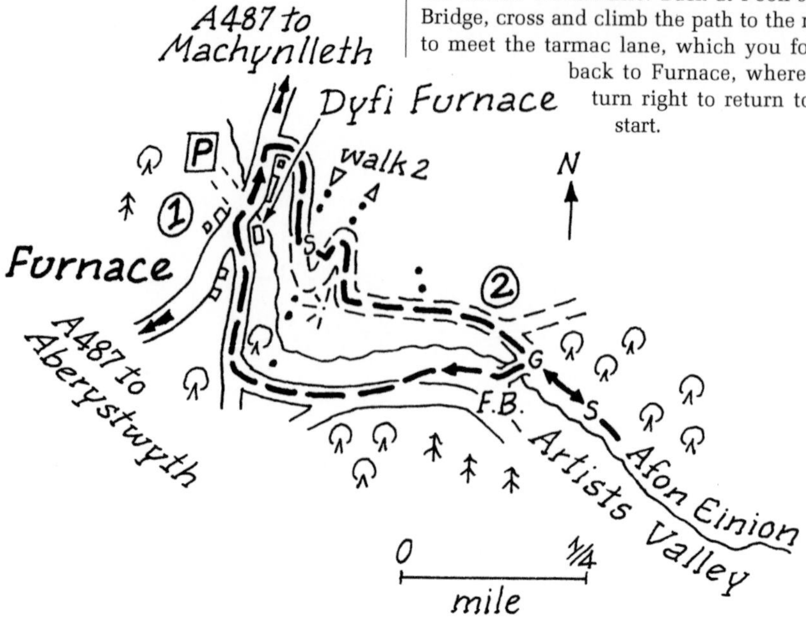

A487 to
Machynlleth

Dyfi Furnace

walk 2

N

Furnace

A487 to
Aberystwyth

F.B.

Artists Valley

Afon Einion

0   ¼

mile

Walk 2

FOEL FAWR

DESCRIPTION Another short walk of 2½ miles along the pleasant hillside of Foel Fawr. The open aspect of the hill gives excellent views of the Dyfi estuary and the hills beyond. A high point of about 325 feet with easy walking, but both the upper and lower parts of the walk can be quite wet underfoot. Allow 1¼ hours.

START Dyfi Furnace car park [SN 685952]

DIRECTIONS Turn west off the A487 in Furnace, just before the river bridge, into the very handy car park.

1 Follow the directions of the previous walk to the seat by the hairpin bend. At the seat, take the waymarked path to the LEFT. Continue along this grassy path. *There are excellent views over the Dyfi estuary to Aberdyfi. On the high ridge behind are the cairns on Trum Gelli and the high points of Tarren Hendre and Tarren y Gesail.*

2 After about ½ mile, the path bears RIGHT, uphill for a few yards, and the markers indicate another right turn, back towards the start of the walk. However, take the path to the LEFT and continue on the original line – north-northwest – until the first chance of a LEFT turn downhill – it is a bit indistinct, but don't worry, the level path soon turns down to meet this one, although this first is the better path.

3 Continue down to pass behind a little stone building and meet tarmac at Melindwr. Turn LEFT, onto the lane. Melindwr is Welsh for watermill and the wheel pit and leat for the mill are further on, round the corner to the right. Carry on along the level lane from Melindwr for 500 yards to a green path, which branches LEFT before a cattle grid. *In the field by the path is a memorial to Major General Lewis Owain Pugh, who served in Burma.* Follow the path, alongside a restored stone wall, for ½ mile. This path runs for a while through a steep-sided, wooded, little valley which in bad weather is often quite wet. At the end of the path the stile is by the cattle grid. Here you turn RIGHT down the lane back to Furnace.

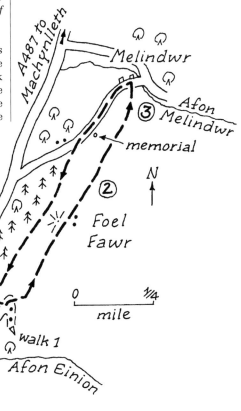

3

Walk 3

LLYN CONACH & NEW POOL VIA CWM EINION

DESCRIPTION A comfortable walk of 7¾ miles on mainly forest and mountain roads, steadily climbing 1500 feet. Largely in the popular Artist's Valley, with splendid views from the high forest and a stroll round three lakes on the plateau. Allow 4½ hours.

START Ystrad Einion car park [SN 708938]

DIRECTIONS Turn east off the A487 in Furnace, just before the river bridge, into a narrow lane signed Artist's Valley. Follow the lane as it climbs alongside the river and past the picnic area for nearly 2 miles to turn off into the parking area over the bridge on the right.

1 Take the forest road from the car park bridge into the forest. *The mine workings above are the preserved remains of Ystrad Einion mine. Above the buildings is the covered engine shaft of massive proportions. Also worth noting are the owl boxes – blue plastic drums – in the trees below the building.* Now take the higher of the two forest roads, just below the buildings, and climb steadily through forest, until a crossroads is reached after ¾ mile. Take the lower of the two roads ahead and continue for a mile or so, rounding the head of the valley, *with views of Cardigan Bay and the hills above Aberdyfi.* Here the road turns round to the north for a short way and passes a quarry. For those who don't mind a scramble, a rough path on the forest side of the LEFT quarry fence can be scaled to gain a gravelly track. This same track can be reached from the main road, some 150 yards beyond the quarry. Either way, follow this track, rising fairly sharply, to the RIGHT (south-east).

2 Soon the standing forest gives way to open clear-cut and the path is less clear. Press on forward for a few yards, keeping close to the left forest edge, to the shore of Llyn Conach, with the dam to the right. *Llyn Conach, the first lake on the Taylor's Leat system, was fed by a leat over a mile long, which, seen on the hillside opposite, collected water from two north-flowing streams and, via the leat system, sent it south! The leat enters Llyn Conach about 50 yards beyond the end of the dam, with the outlet sluice at the near end. Below the dam, in marshy ground, is the smaller pond of Llyn Dwfn. Water from here was led clockwise round the hill to power the wheels in the valley at Esgair Fraith.* Follow the track southeast from the far end of the dam and shortly join a more substantial road from the right.

Go towards the next lake, New Pool, and the fishing lodge of Angler's Retreat. *This modern building is on the site of Plas y Mynydd, the summer residence of the Pryse family. On the mound by the lodge is the pets' graveyard with several headstones. Water from New Pool was discharged into Afon Llechweddmawr and joined the water returning from Esgair Fraith via the Afon Lleustgota, where it entered the main leat system to mines as far south as Cwmbrwyno.*

3 Do not pass New Pool, but take the road to the RIGHT towards the forest,

crossing a bridge to enter the forest through a gate. From the gate follow the rising track and, in less than ½ mile, join the road from Llyn Dwfn. After about 200 yards, just past a road on the left, take the metalled road on the RIGHT, heading north.

4 This road returns you to Cwm Einion at a higher level, with even better views. Continue for about 2 miles to return to the crossroads from instruction **1**, where you take the lower, RIGHT-hand fork and retrace your steps to the start.

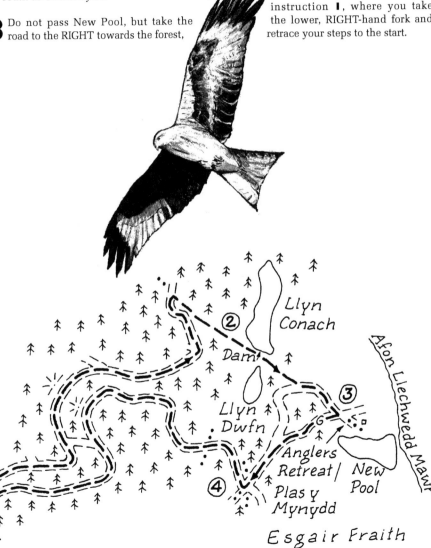

5

Walk 4

BONT-GOCH TO CWMERFYN

DESCRIPTION A 10 mile walk on forest and mountain roads, to a high point of 1250 feet, mostly with gentle gradients but there are two short steep ascents towards the end. With two Iron Age forts, three lakes, numerous mines and stupendous views of deep valleys, this is a very interesting walk – one of my favourites. Allow about 5 hours.

START Road junction south of Bont-goch [SN 677856]

DIRECTIONS Approach Bont-goch from Talybont and the junction is to the south. There is room for one car on the grass verge by the field entrance, opposite the lane end.

Follow the lane, rising slowly, southeast for about ½ mile to Llety Ifan Hen. Leaving the farm entrance on your right, continue a few yards through two gates in succession. At the end of the next field the road divides; take the RIGHT fork through a gate and around the side of the hill, passing an old adit and opening up a good view of the head of the valley. *In the centre of the valley is a small hill, crowned by the Iron Age fort of Pen y Castell. On the far side of the valley the hillside is crossed two leats, which carried water from the Afon Leri to the Cwmsymlog mines.* Continue downhill to a gate, *to the left of which is a gash in the rock, an ancient opencut, where ore was dug out at surface level.* After the gate bear RIGHT to the second gate, cross the dam of the pond and ascend the slope on the other side, passing the Blaencastell Outdoor Activities Centre. *Just before the next gate the track crosses Taylor's Leat, which is most evident on the left hand side and is the higher of the two leats seen crossing the field earlier. Looking back across the valley the workings of Llety Evan Hen can be seen.* Continue up the lane, past the assault course, and take the first path on the RIGHT, winding up through conifers. Cross the tarmac road diagonally LEFT and enter the forest immediately past the cottage.

2 Follow the forest track to join a main forest road, heading slightly south of east. *Through the trees on your right can be seen the village of Cwmsymlog and the remains of the mine with its tottering boiler chimney.* The road reaches the head of the valley and a crossroads. Take the LEFT branch, winding upwards through old mine workings. *This is Blaen Cwmsymlog, which, in the 1620s, returned £24,000 annually in silver – then an immense fortune! Look out for an old shaft on the left.* The sloping track rises to Llyn Pendam and joins the tarmac. Turn RIGHT and walk clockwise round the lake, turning LEFT at the next junction and following the road through the trees to Llyn Blaenmelindwr. Just before reaching the dam, turn RIGHT through a gate onto a mountain road, which runs above the valley. *As the road rises gently an old leat can be seen*

To Talybo

to Bow Street

Llety Ifan l

Troedrhiws

F.B

N

Salem

0 ¼ mile

Pen-rhiw-newydd

Nant Silo

Darren Bank

Fort

Darer

④

6

crossing the route, at one time carrying water from Llyn Rhosgoch, on the right, to mines ahead.

3 Crossing the ridge, the road surface deteriorates, with mine workings on our left. The panoramic view of Cwmerfyn, with the numerous workings far below, and the Iron Age fort of Darren in the left distance soon make up for the poor road. Carry on past the capped shafts with their pillbox like structures – the metal grills allowing access for the bat population – and cross the tarmac road from the valley to pass through the gate opposite. Follow the path by the trees and, after a slight left-hand bend, enter the forest, turning RIGHT onto the main forest road, to contour the hill. *As the trees thin out, views of the Goginan valley open to the left.* Leaving the corner of the forest, keep on the road, ignoring footpaths, until the surface changes to tarmac in a few hundred yards at Banc-y-Darren. *Beyond the cottages, the workings of Darren mine are evident. The mineral vein must have been cut*

and worked by the builders of the hill fort over two thousand years ago, as it passes through the ramparts. However, the great trench running up the hill from your left is Roman.

4 Turn RIGHT at the next crossroads, pass the house called Darren Bank, and, where the road turns sharp right, cross the stile ahead. Go down the fields, keeping RIGHT of the fence. At the bottom, cross another stile into a small lane and turn RIGHT. In a few yards turn LEFT at the public road and cross the river bridge. Take the bridleway on your RIGHT and climb a steep diagonal, past old adits, to Pen-rhiw-newydd. Take the public road straight ahead, ignoring the farm road to the right, and descend steeply to the village of Salem, where, at the corner you turn diagonally RIGHT, away from the main road, down to farm buildings on the left. Cross a sometimes-tied gate to the RIGHT of the cottage ahead and follow the green road with the field boundary on your LEFT until the boundary (possibly just old posts at this point), turns LEFT and follow the fence line down to the spinney. Find the path through the spinney to the footbridge over the stream and climb up the far bank, crossing the gate between the house of Troedrhiwseiri and the out-building. At the far side of this tiny paddock leave by the gate and turn RIGHT, up the house drive, to join a sharply rising road. After a couple of hundred yards, pass through the gate at the end of the road and turn LEFT and so back to the start.

ont goch pond

Pen y Castell Blaencastell

Cwmsymlog

Llyn Pendam

Llyn Blaenmelindwr Dam

Llyn Rhosgoch

Cwmferyn

TALYBONT TO BRYN ARIAN MINE

DESCRIPTION A short walk of 4¾ miles along a pleasant lane, through fields and forest tracks, climbing to a high point of 660 feet. Pass the remains of several mines, with views over the SSSI of Borth Bog to the sea. The turning point of the walk is at the impressive stonework of Bryn Arian mine. After a descent through the wooded mine workings there is a level mile of forest road back to the top of the village. Allow 2 hours.

START Talybont village green [SN 655893]

I Take the lane to the RIGHT of the Black Lion Hotel and, after a few hundred yards, take the smaller lane to the LEFT of the large Victorian semis. After a similar distance, the Afon Ceulan is crossed by a bridge, just before farm buildings on the right. At the junction ahead turn RIGHT. Soon after the last bungalow on the left and beyond a field gate is a signed public footpath, which turns back to skirt the edge of the forest and rise into the field. *The lanes walked to this point are said to be part of Sarn Helen, a road system developed in Roman times, running up the length of Wales. It is probable that the basic route is much older but was upgraded from track to road by the Romans. I have personally dug through the road surface south of the river bridge and, at that point, a thin layer of tarmac covers a base of large cobbles, whether Roman or not is hard to tell! The road is thought to be named after Helen, the British wife of the Roman commander who constructed the highway. To the locals, the British woman was the big cheese, not the Roman commander!* Follow the path uphill and contour clockwise round the field, above the single tree but below the two tree-guarded shafts on the right, with more workings of Penpompren mine on the right skyline.

2 At the way-marker post to the RIGHT of the gate, the rather vague path becomes a definite road and continues northwards, with views over Borth Bog to the sea. Where the wheel tracks bear right, go straight on to the stream, cross the stile and head diagonally uphill to find the next stile. *The large opencuts of Erglodd mine are evident on the left (not to be confused with the farm of the same name at the bottom of the hill). Ancient stone tools have been found in these workings.* As the stile is crossed, the waste tip from Pen-y-banc mine is on your right. Continue ahead, up the ridge on the LEFT towards a marker post at the end of the ridge and then on to the next post, where you join the track to the ruins of Cefn-erglodd, *with good views behind to the south.* The right of way passes via stiles through the back yard of the old farm. After the far stile, bear slightly RIGHT to the old hedgerow. Follow this, rising slightly, for 150 yards, to a small bog. Skirt the bog anti-clockwise to take the stile behind, turn sharp LEFT for a few yards and then RIGHT up the small valley to the marker post on the skyline to the right of the hawthorn. From the post, follow the direction of the arrow, slightly LEFT, to enter the dip beyond the trees on the small ridge to your left and before the fence ahead. A few yards down the dip a stile crosses the fence into the next field. Across the stile, head for the gate at the far end of the field, with a large fenced shaft to the right of the gate.

3 Once through the gate, follow the wheel tracks to the buildings of Bryn Arian mine. *This solid structure consists of a substantial wheel pit situated between two working areas, one of which must have housed the ore crushers.* This is the turning point of the walk. Now retrace your steps along the wheel track south-westerly away from the Bryn Arian reservoir, down the field. Where the wheel tracks bear left, back towards the gate, go RIGHT towards a dip to the edge of the forest, passing through the waste tips and blocked adits of the mine. Below the main workings, cross a stile in the trees. The track becomes steeper, passing an old, fenced-off shaft on the left. Cross the forest road and take the signed footpath down the bank at

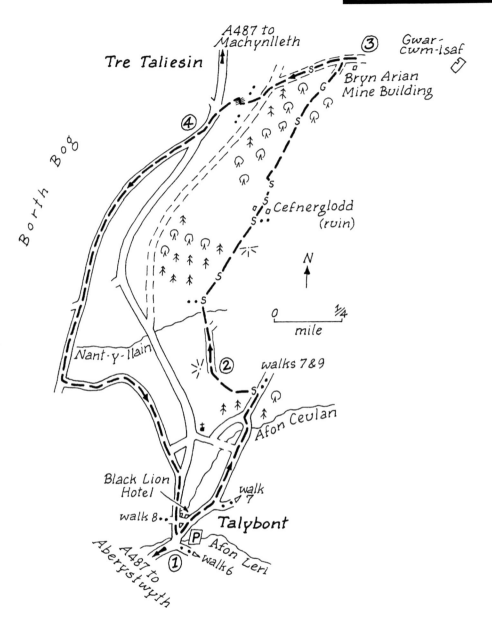

the other side to soon join a path coming from the RIGHT and in a few yards turn RIGHT down a set of steps. The steps lead to a lane, which, in about 25 yards, meets a larger lane. Turn LEFT and descend a short way to the main road.

4 Cross the main road and turn LEFT and, in 150 yards, bear right into a lane, which rises gently for 1¼ miles. Take the first LEFT turn and drop slowly to the village of Talybont in ½ mile. Turn RIGHT in the village and head back to the green.

9

BRAICH GARW, CEFN GWYN & THE WINDMILLS

DESCRIPTION 6¼ miles of easy walking, along quiet lanes, forest tracks and fields, to a high point of 900 feet. Here, in spite of its relatively low altitude, there are some of the best views in the area. You can examine the remains of old technology and rub shoulders with the latest means of power generation – a good chance to decide which side you are on in the wind power debate! Time spent exploring Cefn Gwyn, in its peaceful valley, shows how gracefully nature can reclaim its own. Allow 3 hours.
START Talybont Village Green [SN 655893]

I Walk south from the green in Talybont and take the first turn LEFT up a narrow lane, in front of the hairdresser's at Salon Leri. Continue up the lane, with open fields on the right and, after the last bungalow, trees coming in on the left. *A small, red brick building can been seen in the trees below, which once housed the village generator, powered by a water wheel. An embankment in the fields on the right indicates the old route of the Hafan tramway.* After ½ mile, the road passes through a gate and also crosses the Hafan trackbed, which runs on the level by the river, up the valley. Follow the unfenced road upwards, with the slopes of Braich Garw on the right. As the trees start to close in again, cross a stream and cattle grid, and pass a large beef shed on the left. Soon the road turns sharp RIGHT and rises a short way to Pen-y-bontbren-uchaf. Walk up between the house and the buildings – *beware of the dogs* – and, at the top of the slope, take the LEFT hand gate out of the farm.

2 Follow this track, inside the forest edge, for ½ mile, until the fields on the left give way to trees and the track climbs to a stile over the LEFT hand fence. Cross the stile and take the narrow path across the wooded hillside until another stile leads onto open ground. Follow the more difficult path, through bracken, dropping towards the river. Go over the next stile. *The remains of Cefn Gwyn mine are in front and a footbridge spans the river. Before crossing the river, explore the workings on the surface in this peaceful valley. Look for adits on both sides of the river. There is a wheel pit and crusher house with its sandy waste, and the main rubbish runs.* Cross the footbridge. *Look for*

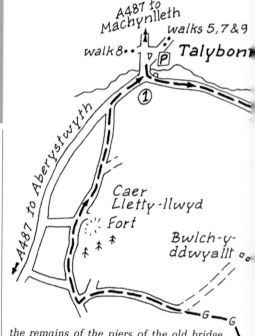

the remains of the piers of the old bridge, which carried the mine tramway across the river from the two adits on the north bank.

3 From the footbridge, climb the steep slope with a hairpin bend at the top; bear LEFT to the next gate at the right of the buildings, then down the drive of Plas Cefn Gwyn to the road. Turn RIGHT. A short way after the next bungalow a rough track drops away RIGHT towards farm buildings. Follow this through the gate at the bottom, then take the track to the LEFT to meet the river at a ford and footbridge, above a waterfall. *Look downstream from the bridge to the right bank and try to spot the iron bar,* with a hooked end, sticking out of the rock. This bracket supported the wooden box-work, or launder, which carried water from above the fall to the wheels at Cefn Gwyn. After the bridge, pass through the gate and climb up the bank into the open field. Bear LEFT, through the boggy ground, heading for the track between the rising ground and the fence. Just before a stile over the fence on the left, with a copse of trees and another stile ahead, the track branches RIGHT and climbs sharply to a T-junction.

4 At the junction, ignore the right and left tracks and take the footpath indicated on the marker, up the field ahead to the stile in the LEFT hand corner. The route for the next mile is by obvious way-marked stiles and

gates, passing a place where farm machinery goes to die, and rising gently to the top of the hill. The route is repeatedly crossed by the service tracks for the windmills, which are now all around. *If any of the service engineers are present, they are always very helpful and only too happy to tell you about the turbines. The panoramic views from this section of the walk are worthy of much higher mountains and make this small climb doubly worthwhile. Further along the ridge to the east are the remains of Pen Dinas iron-age fort.*

5 Just below the top of the hill, pass through a bridle gate, which is just to the right of a gate on the service track. Turn LEFT across the service road and walk into the small valley, avoiding the boggy bits, to the bridle gate at the left hand end of the next cross fence. Continue down the gently sloping valley to pass through the bridle gate in the unfinished fence on your RIGHT. Pass below the old mine scrape and curve round to the far right corner of the field, through the gate and straight on to the next gate. In the next field, the route joins the concrete road from Bwlch-y-ddwyallt, which is followed until it meets a tarred lane. Turn right for Talybont, ¾ mile away, and, in a few yards, pass below the ramparts of Caer Lletty-llwyd iron-age fort. Carry on until the lane meets the main road and walk with care downhill to the village green.

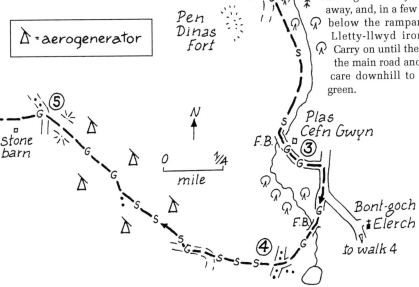

11

Walk 7

CWM CEULAN & CWM EINION FROM TALYBONT

DESCRIPTION A walk of 12 miles to a high point of 1500 feet at a col below the summit of Moel-y-llyn, over quiet lanes and mountain road, returning by a forest road and the delightful Cwm Einion. Allow 5 hours.

START Talybont Village Green [SN 655893]

I From the green, take the Bont-goch road by the Black Lion, follow round to the RIGHT in front of the Victorian semis and turn LEFT below the bungalows, soon passing the farm of Neuadd-fawr, *where, when the leaves are off the hedge, the old farm machinery waterwheel can be seen on the left.* From the farm, the road continues eastwards, in trees, for 1¼ miles, past an old quarry, and the narrow valley of the Afon Ceulan slowly opens out. After open fields, the road re-enters the forest for a few yards and, after the trees, soon take a LEFT fork by a cattle grid.

2 Avoid the left turn to Carregcadwgan and go slightly downhill for a 200 yards, to a sharp LEFT turn, then RIGHT by a caravan field. You soon pass a converted chapel, with a nursery, and go through a gate. Carry on, avoiding the drive to Rhyd-yr-onen on the left, and take the LEFT of the two gates ahead. The route, now a green mountain road, bears away left and it can be seen how much the valley has widened since Neuadd-fawr. Climb steadily for just over a mile, with the slopes of Moel y Llyn on your left.

3 When the road reaches the col, pass through the forest gate, descend the rough, rocky track to the forest road and turn LEFT. After ½ mile, at the crossroads, take the lower, RIGHT-hand, road and keep on the forest road for a mile to the old mine and car park at Ystrad Einion. Turn LEFT out of the

car park onto the minor road and follow the tarmac for 1¾ miles down the delightful valley, keeping company with the river all the way. Just after a footpath sign on the right, an un-surfaced lane leaves the road on the LEFT and runs between fields and the forest for ¼ mile, through a gate, to a cross roads at the house called Coed Garth.

4 Turn LEFT at the crossroads and take the green lane for ¼ mile to the next crossroads at Llwyn-gwyn, and go straight across. Continue to follow the green lane for nearly a mile, passing through a gate to join the tarmac road at a tight bend. Take the LEFT leg of the road and go for about 3 miles, crossing the Afon Cletwr in its small valley before passing Gwar-cwm-uchaf and climbing out of the valley to excellent views to the west, along the lane to Pen-y-sarn-ddu and Cwmslaid, to the outskirts of Talybont. Take the first turn LEFT, signed to Nant-y-moch, and carry on the ½ mile back to the village green.

Bedd Taliesin

Cw. Slai

Walk 5

Black Lion Hotel

Neuadc Fawr

walk 8

Aberystwyth

A487 to

P *Talybont*

walk 6

12

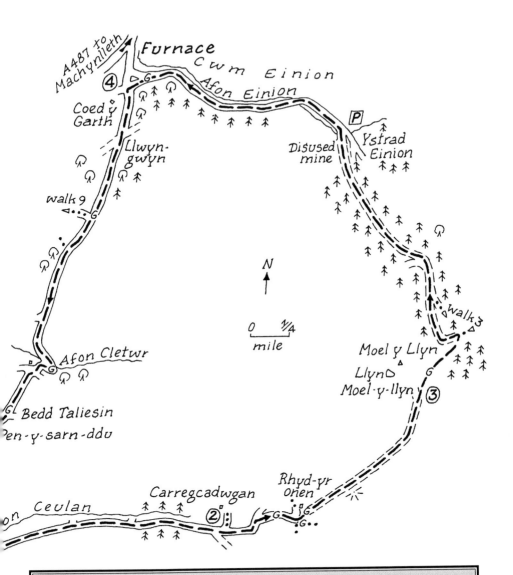

A487 to Machynlleth

Furnace

Cwm Einion

Afon Einion

④

Coed y Garth

Llwyn-gwyn

walk 9

Disused mine

P

Ystrad Einion

N

0   ¼
mile

Afon Cletwr

Bedd Taliesin

Pen-y-sarn-ddu

Moel y Llyn

Llyn

Moel-y-llyn

③

walk 3

Carregcadwgan

②

Rhyd-yr onen

on Ceulan

Roger Handley was raised in Cumbria and as a child roamed the fells above Morcambe Bay. A working life based in Manchester allowed ready access to the Lake District, encouraged by membership of the Crown Paints Walking Club. After a golden handshake in 1985, he and his wife purchased a caravan park near Talybont and soon learned to love this area of Wales. The sale of the park in 1992 allowed the freedom to explore the local hills and to really appreciate the peaceful solitude available within a couple of miles of the back door – a complete contrast to the crowded Lake District.

Walk 8

TALYBONT TO BORTH

DESCRIPTION A low-level walk of about 7 miles, on forest roads and lanes, with a chance to sample the delights of the seaside. A short section crosses the re-claimed part of Borth Bog and, from the slightly higher ground, extensive views are to be had of the hills around the Dyfi estuary. Allow 3½ hours – or longer if a refreshment stop is taken in Borth.
START Talybont Village Green [SN 655893]

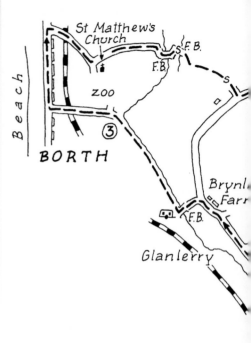

I With the pubs on your RIGHT hand side, cross the green and the main road and enter the lane opposite, leading up towards the forest. Bear LEFT at the junction by the monkey-puzzle tree and climb gently to the forest gate in 300 yards. Through the gate, follow the forest road, ignoring all byroads on the right, for a mile to the far end of the forest, with the Afon Leri on your left all the way. Through the gate, head slightly uphill across the field, aiming for the gap between the oaks on the left and the gorse on the right. Cross into the next field and to the ruins of Fron-gôch farm, passing between the buildings and the house. Do not take the track on the left but head up hill to the far top corner of the field and so into the next field. Follow the LEFT hand fence along the hillside to cross the next dilapidated fence and carry on to a stile and bridle gate, side by side, at the end of the third field. Over the stile bear RIGHT and follow the fence upwards, ignoring the gate into the field on the left, and passing through the gate by the water trough behind the farm buildings of Henllys. In a few yards, take the gate on the LEFT into the drive from the farm and turn RIGHT to the lane.

2 Turn LEFT and follow the lane to the T-junction by the old house and more modern bungalow. Turn LEFT and almost immediately RIGHT. Follow the new lane for ½ mile, past Tai-canol, to Brynllys Farm, where, just beyond the farm, you turn LEFT past a shingled bungalow. The road crosses

a stream and stops at a gateway on the right; bear LEFT to a footbridge over the Afon Leri, onto Glanlerry Caravan Park. Turn RIGHT and walk along the embankment of the river for ½ mile to the Animalarium (zoo) at Borth.

3 At the Zoo turn LEFT and carry on along the tarmac road, over the level crossing, into Borth – *with the opportunity – very rare on these walks – of sampling the hospitality of one of the pubs.* To return to the route, walk north through Borth, and 600 yards from where you joined the main street, just after the houses cease on the left, take the small turning on the RIGHT, signed to *St Matthew's Church.* Follow the lane to the church, which sits on a rocky outcrop surrounded by reclaimed bog, and at the church take the LEFT fork through the gate by the churchyard. Walk east for 600 yards to the bank of the Afon Leri, then turn RIGHT by the sewage works to a footbridge over the river. Turn LEFT off the bridge and, after a few yards, bear RIGHT down the embankment to a stile and another footbridge over a ditch. Follow the fence away from the river

14

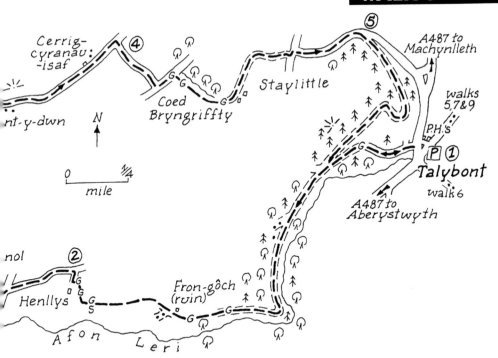

to a white-topped post, then bear LEFT to another white-topped post at the far side of the peaty field. Cross the stile into the short lane by the farm building and turn LEFT at the end onto tarmac. After 300 yards you reach Pant-y-dwn, *with extensive views over the bog to the Dyfi estuary and the hills beyond.* At the farm pass the buildings and stay on the lane, do not take the footpath going up hill, and in ½ mile you come to Cerrig-cyranau-isaf, where you again stay on the lane, avoiding the footpath signed down to the left.

4 In another 300 yards you come to a T-junction and turn RIGHT for ¼ mile to the next junction, where you turn LEFT and walk towards the small wood on the right of the road. Just before the wood take the gate into the field and then take the gate into the wood, Coed Bryngriffty, a few yards up the field. Follow the stream through the trees and head for the left-hand corner of the garden fence of the cottage ahead, and follow the fence to the gate into the lane.

Carry on LEFT along the lane to the junction in Staylittle and turn LEFT, then, after a few yards, turn RIGHT.

5 In another ¼ mile, past a small cottage with a large greenhouse, take the forest road on the RIGHT with the red barrier, and climb gently for ¼ mile or so. The road takes a sweep round to the RIGHT, by a shale bank, above which is an ancient open cut, to face some old spoil heaps. Just before the spoil heaps a wide forest road goes off to the LEFT and drops down towards the village. Follow this road and, in a few yards, cross the top of some large spoil heaps, revealing a viewpoint above the trees. *Up the bank to the right of the road, amongst the gorse bushes, is a fenced adit, which, especially in warm weather, can have a blast of air rising from deep in the hill.* Downhill from the adit you soon reach a red barrier and, immediately afterwards, turn LEFT to drop down to the lowest forest road, where you turn LEFT again to retrace the route back to the village.

TALIESIN'S GRAVE VIA SARN HELEN

DESCRIPTION A walk of just over 7 miles, for the first half along a lane said to be the old Roman road of Sarn Helen as described in **Walk 6**, visiting the grave of the bard Taliesin – or so tradition has it – en route. There are excellent views of the Dyfi estuary and the peaks to Cadair Idris from several points on the way. You return through two forest sections and pass through the village of Tre'r-ddôl where refreshment is available at the Wildfowler Inn. The highest point is only 700 feet and the whole route is easy walking. Allow 3¼ hours.
START Talybont village green [SN 655893]

Take the lane to the RIGHT of the Black Lion Hotel and, after a few hundred yards, take the smaller lane to the LEFT of the large Victorian semis. After a similar distance, the Afon Ceulan is crossed by a bridge, just before farm buildings on the right. At the T-junction ahead turn RIGHT and follow the lane, round a dogleg with the tips of Rhyd-fach mine in the trees on the left, for about a mile to the next dogleg just past the bungalow of Penrhos on the right, at the farm of Pen-y-sarn-ddu. *Before turning RIGHT into the dogleg, take in the view ahead over the Dyfi estuary as far as Cadair Idris and look down the left turn, which is the drive to Gwar-cwm-isaf, to see the remains of Pensarn mine. The stone structure on the right of the lane is the wheel pit, constructed in 1869 at a cost of a halfcrown a cubic yard, including materials!*

2 Continue to the RIGHT, through the gate and, *before turning left, notice the old chapel by the farm and wonder – why here?* Turn LEFT out of the dogleg and before the next gate, examine the grassy area on the right where a mountain road leaves the lane. *There are two or three low stony mounds, the*

furthest of which can be seen to be a shallow stone chamber, with one of the roof stones still evident, all surrounded by earth. This is traditionally Bedd Taliesin or Taliesin's Grave. Back on the lane, continue for 500 yards to Gwar-cwm-uchaf, where you start to descend sharply to the gorge of the Afon Cletwr. At the bottom, cross the gated bridge, climb up the lane *and notice the remains of the original road and bridge in the gorge below.* Carry on for ¾ mile, ignoring the lane going left, passing the remains of Ynystudor mine in the wood on the left, until you reach a U-bend in the road, where the tarmac goes left and Sarn Helen continues ahead as a green lane.

3 Follow the tarmac, as you turn for home, through the farm of Cefnweiriog and downhill for another ½ mile, until a forest road, with a red barrier, goes off to the LEFT. Take this road, which soon narrows to a path, down the hillside for just over ½ mile to join the main road in Tre'r-ddôl. *Before going through the gate onto the road, notice the fenced adit on your right, which is the remains of Tre'r-ddol mine, which is interesting because there are two different adits joining at the entrance.*

4 After passing through the gate, walk towards the garage and bear LEFT into the village, soon passing the Wildfowler Inn on your right. At the far end of the village, take the lane on the LEFT alongside the church and bear RIGHT around the back of the church to turn LEFT up the hill in an old muddy lane. After the last bungalow on the left, the lane branches RIGHT through a field gate and continues to climb towards the forest. At the forest gate, take the RIGHT turn onto the path, which, at the next gate, enters the turning area at the end of a forest road. A path leaves the turning area on the right and carries on, alongside the field fence, for 700 yards, to be joined by a path from the left and, in a couple of yards, to pass above a set of steps. The path climbs gently up the bank to meet the forest road, which you cross and take the steeper ride on the other side. After 50 yards or so cross a small ride as the path steepens to meet a marker post where

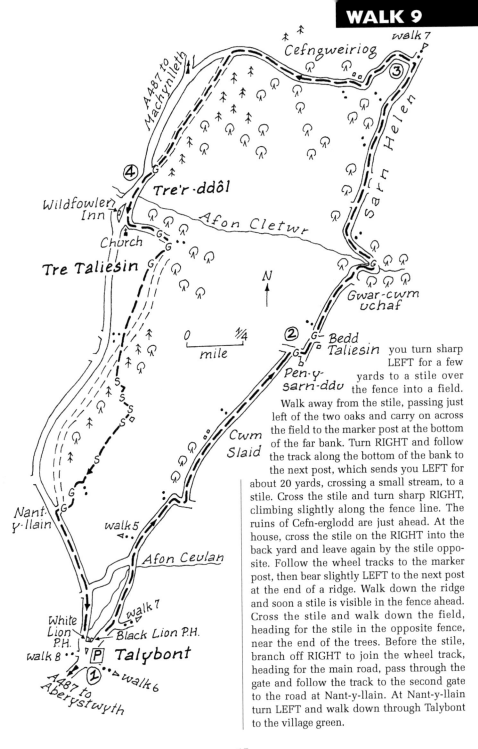

Cefngweiriog

walk 7

3

Sarn Helen

A487 to Machynlleth

4

Tre'r·ddôl

Wildfowler Inn

Church

Tre Taliesin

Afon Cletwr

N

0   ¼
mile

Gwar-cwm uchaf

2 Bedd **Taliesin** you turn sharp LEFT for a few yards to a stile over **Pen-y-sarn-ddu** the fence into a field.

Cwm Slaid

Nant y-llain

walk 5

Afon Ceulan

White Lion P.H.

Black Lion P.H.

walk 7

P **Talybont**

walk 8

1 *walk 6*

A487 to Aberystwyth

Walk away from the stile, passing just left of the two oaks and carry on across the field to the marker post at the bottom of the far bank. Turn RIGHT and follow the track along the bottom of the bank to the next post, which sends you LEFT for about 20 yards, crossing a small stream, to a stile. Cross the stile and turn sharp RIGHT, climbing slightly along the fence line. The ruins of Cefn-erglodd are just ahead. At the house, cross the stile on the RIGHT into the back yard and leave again by the stile opposite. Follow the wheel tracks to the marker post, then bear slightly LEFT to the next post at the end of a ridge. Walk down the ridge and soon a stile is visible in the fence ahead. Cross the stile and walk down the field, heading for the stile in the opposite fence, near the end of the trees. Before the stile, branch off RIGHT to join the wheel track, heading for the main road, pass through the gate and follow the track to the second gate to the road at Nant-y-llain. At Nant-y-llain turn LEFT and walk down through Talybont to the village green.

17

Walk 10

THE RHEIDOL VALLEY, CWMBRWYNO & JUBILEE WALK

DESCRIPTION An 8½-mile walk on lanes and forest roads, with some field paths. The route initially climbs steadily, with a level section, a gentle descent and a steep section at the end before dropping down to the start. Good views from the ridge and the forest route. Allow 4 hours.

START Lay by in Cwm Rheidol [SN 681792]

DIRECTIONS Turn south off the A44 in Capel Bangor into Cwm Rheidol, drive 1½ miles to a lay by on the right, with a post box.

I Walk on a few yards to take the lane to Tycam, rising gently past the farm. Cross the ford at Neuadd Parc, on a stony track, under trees, to a second ford, ignoring the footpath on the left. Shortly, the now grassy track passes a pond and enters a meadow, keeping RIGHT by the trees, to leave at the top corner and enter the oaks. Leaving the wood by the second gate, carry on past Hafodau Cottage, until you have to turn RIGHT to a gate by the ruins of Gwarllyn. The lane, now on open ground, *with views of the Rheidol Valley*, bears LEFT to the ruins of Gelli, LEFT again round the old buildings and crosses the ridge to meet tarmac at the crossroads at Pen-rhiwlas, some 1½ miles from Tycam. *From the ridge, the view to the right opens into a high valley, with the hill fort of Castell Bwa-drain in the middle distance.*

2 At the crossroads go straight ahead and soon, on the left, *the Cwmbrwyno valley is spread out below, with the 'landscaped' Cwmbrwyno mine. This mine is the southernmost served by Taylor's Leat, which crosses the opposite hillside.* Follow the road to the end of the valley, towards the wind turbines of Ystumtuen. Take the public footpath, ¼ mile after the Ystumtuen road branches right,

over a stile on the LEFT, just after a cattle grid, walking slightly back, over a second stile, towards Cwmbrwyno, then over a small ridge, until a dip in the ground allows an easy stroll to the RIGHT to the main A44. Cross the road to the Nantyrarian Visitor Centre car parks, rather than dropping down to the café. *However, if you are here at about 14.00 (GMT), the local red kites will be dining at the feeding station by the lake.*

3 At the end of the top car park, take the path to the LEFT, past the picnic tables and down steps, curving RIGHT to carry on above the deep valley below. *This level path is part of the Jubilee Walk from the Visitor Centre; however, its history goes back almost 160 years, as this is the Cwmbrwyno branch of Taylor's Leat. In places you can make out the ditch on the right of the path.* Follow the leat for about a mile, with views of the hillside across the valley. *Notice the two old leats running at different levels on the open hillside. The higher is from Llyn Rhosgoch and the lower is the Goginan branch of Taylor's Leat, which served mines on the ridge and in Goginan.* When the path joins a forest road, turn LEFT and head back south, with the road eventually curving round to the west. After a mile, just before the road doglegs right over a bridge, *the old Level Newydd mine workings are seen on the right bank of the river. Doubling back just over the bridge, a small diversion takes you to some ruined buildings, with a collapsing wheel pit on the right, which was served by a leat from up-stream.* Back on the route, the forest soon gives way to fields on the left and, *just before the fields, you pass an old adit, now fenced across, on the right.* The forest road curves round the fields towards the south and, after 600 yards, turns west again.

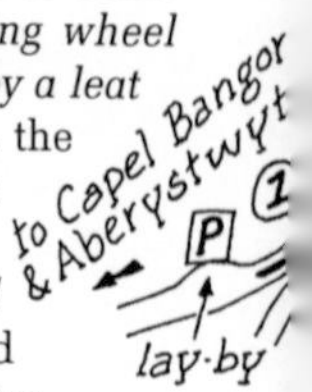

4 At this point turn LEFT at a minor crossroads and soon, where the road bears right, go straight ahead, down steps, onto a sometimes way-marked footpath – the short post tends to fall over! The path crosses the fence and heads south, over a footbridge, follows the field fence and crosses a small ford to a stile, then up the right of the field, to a gate into the road. Follow the road west, take the RIGHT fork through the gate by the barn at the junction, turn LEFT at the road into the village of Goginan and, by the first old chapel, turn LEFT again. In a few yards the road bears RIGHT. Go through the higher field gate on the LEFT to follow the old hedgerow up the field, through the hedge into the second field and diagonally upwards to the churchyard gate at the top corner.

5 Cross the main road and take the lane opposite. Climb past a few houses, round a dogleg, and, after ¼ mile, turn sharp RIGHT. Keep on the level road, past the house of Llwyn-gwyn, until a bridleway sign directs you through a gate and a short way anti-clockwise round a mound, through a gap in the fence, to follow the markers for a few yards to a another gate into the forest on the left. Bear RIGHT here, through the second gate and descend the grassy track to the RIGHT, to reach the edge of a small field, where you bear LEFT. After a few yards ford the stream in the dip through gates and, bearing right, follow the path down to another small gate, carrying on until a gate opens onto the stony track to Tycam, where you turn right to retrace your steps for about ½ mile to the start.

CWM RHEIDOL, THE MYNACH VALLEY & PARSON'S BRIDGE

DESCRIPTION A walk of 8¼ miles, crossing the Rheidol and Mynach gorges. You follow a steep forest path, then through fields round Devil's Bridge, down to the Mynach. From here you climb, on paths and forest roads, to your high point of 1300 feet, before dropping by mountain road to the gorge of the Rheidol, then climbing gradually to Ystumtuen and down by forest road to return to the start. Allow about 4½ hours.

START Cwm Rheidol Filter Beds [SN 727782]

DIRECTIONS From the A44 in Capel Bangor, turn south to Cwm Rheidol. After about five miles, a blue sign indicates the filter beds. Park on the right.

1 Cross the Rheidol by the footbridge, below the rapids, and bear LEFT, to climb a short way up the field to a gate into the trees. Through the gate, take the lower LEFT path for 300 yards, with views of the river and Cwm Rheidol mine, until a marker points RIGHT to a narrower path which climbs steadily through the trees to the track of the Rheidol Railway. Follow the waymarks and cross the track three times to end on the south side. Turn LEFT. After 50 yards, pass through a gate, bear RIGHT up the hill, then walk clockwise around a group of trees, onto a good path, rising slowly, through oaks to meet a green road, where you turn LEFT. Follow this around the trees to a gate to the right of the houses.

2 Turn LEFT into the road towards Devil's Bridge, and then RIGHT at the next junction. After ¼ mile, when the road kinks left to the school, go through the gate between the bungalow and the schoolhouse and follow this gated lane across fields for ½ mile,

passing Rhos-tyddyn farm, until the main road is approached near a bungalow. At the end of the bungalow's fence, turn sharp LEFT to cross a stile into the drive and then turn RIGHT to the road. Turn RIGHT, *with views of the Mynach valley to the left,* and, shortly, take the gate on the LEFT, labeled *'No longer a RUPP'.* Immediately take the waymarked path LEFT, to a footbridge over the Mynach and the ruins of a mill. *The tailrace of the mill can be seen in the stonework of the far bank and the wheel pit is at the back of the site.* Follow the marker on the LEFT at the far side. Cross the stile into the field and walk uphill, northwards, left of the rocks, to a way-marked stile by a gate into a green lane. Follow the lane LEFT (northwards), for ½ mile, and turn RIGHT at a marker by the edge of the trees. The next marker is a few yards uphill and, in sight, another marker points RIGHT, up the hillside. The actual path is a little below this marker but soon a post is visible on the ridge. Pass to the RIGHT of the post and contour LEFT to the next marker, where you take a narrow path, through bracken, downhill towards the trees, *with the Mynach valley and Bodcoll mine, at its height in the 1870s,* to your right. The path enters tall trees for ¼ mile and leaves by a stile to a road, which crosses open ground to re-enter trees after the ruins of Llaneithyr. Here you take the LEFT fork, rising anticlockwise for ¾ mile, to the head of a gully, to again fork LEFT. Still climbing, you meet a T-junction, where you turn RIGHT for 400 yards, until a rough path comes up from the right and crosses left to a narrower path. Turn LEFT here and climb for ¼ mile to a gate in the fence.

3 Leave the forested Mynach valley through this gate, *to look down a bare valley towards the wind turbines at Ystumtuen.* Follow the mountain road for a mile past the farm of Tymawr, to the main road, where you turn LEFT for 300 yards before turning RIGHT to the church at Ysbyty Cynfyn. *This old church has an unusual, circular, churchyard wall, incorporating several standing stones, said to be pre-Christian.* Go anticlockwise round the churchyard, through gates, to a green lane,

to Capel Bangor

①

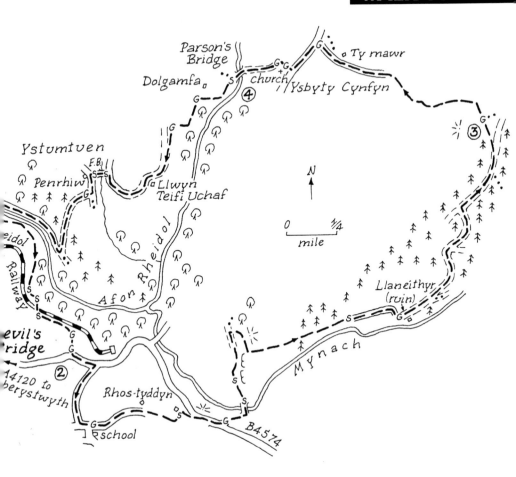

which leads through fields, to the edge of the Rheidol gorge. Follow the steep, zigzag path to Parson's Bridge, *where the vicar from Ystumtuen crossed the river to take services at the church in Ysbyty Cynfyn, saving many miles by road.*

4 Cross the bridge and go LEFT, soon crossing a stile, ignoring the right turn, through the trees to a field below Dolgamfa. Here the footpath has been diverted round the perimeter of the field and leaves through a gate, to join a green track, which crosses a couple more fields, before bearing RIGHT to a post in the field and thence to a gate at the far corner. Through the gate, you soon join a more definite lane to the farm of Llwyn Teifi Uchaf. Follow the lane round to the RIGHT and look out for the farm of Penrhiw on the other side of the valley. As you draw level with the buildings of Penrhiw, cross a stile to a footbridge and climb up to another stile onto the lane by the farm buildings. Turn LEFT and follow the lane southwards for 200 yards to a pair of gates. Take the RIGHT-hand gate, looking into the Rheidol Valley, and follow the steep mountain road towards the river and a road running along the valley. Turn RIGHT for almost ½ mile, passing the Cwm Rheidol mine and returning to your starting point.

Walk 12

THE LLYFNANT VALLEY

DESCRIPTION A low-level walk of 5 miles in a delightful valley, which is one of the un-sung gems of the area. The outward route follows a tarmac road, which undulates along a steep-sided valley, under trees, alongside a mountain stream. The return journey is by forest track and field path, which can be quite muddy in wet weather. There are a couple of adits to look at and lots of opportunities to take photos of the babbling brook. Allow 2½ hours.

START Lay-by on the A487 [SN 703975]

DIRECTIONS Drive north from Talybont through Furnace and Eglwys Fach and 1½ miles beyond Eglwys Fach, after a large corrugated iron shed on the left, park in the lay-by, just beyond the Powys sign.

Walk back from the lay-by and take the un-signed lane on the LEFT, which you follow eastwards for 2½ miles. After 600 yards of almost level road, take the RIGHT fork and climb past the farm of Caerhedyn, with the river below and views ahead into the valley. In another ½ mile, you have trees on both sides and have climbed the valley side to leave the river far below. Carry on along the undulating road until the river is alongside.

2 *At this point notice the flooded adit on the right of the road.* You are now ½ mile from the settlement of Glaspwll, where the road bends round to the LEFT and climbs a few yards to a junction. Turn LEFT at the junction and almost immediately turn down by the phone box towards the white building in front of the barns. You have now turned for home.

3 Take the muddy lane to the RIGHT of the buildings and pass through the gates and a few yards of field, to climb the lane towards the forest. At the forest edge turn RIGHT and follow the track, anticlockwise, round the forest to pass behind the cottage of Gelli-gau. Soon you reach a field gate, where you turn half-RIGHT across the field to gates beyond the power pole. Pass through the LEFT hand gate, onto a forest path, ignoring the left branch, and soon meet another track coming in from the right. Turn RIGHT onto this track and, in less than 100 yards, leave the forest by a gate. The track curves left for about 100 yards, through a field to a large beech tree, where you turn RIGHT for a few yards to a gate into the grounds of the large house of Garthgwynion. Just beyond the gate pass through empty stone gateposts and bear LEFT before the house to follow the drive, besides the beech hedge, to the end of a lane. Cross the lane, bearing slightly RIGHT, and take the green lane opposite, which rises slightly for about 100 yards alongside an overgrown tennis court and gardens. As the

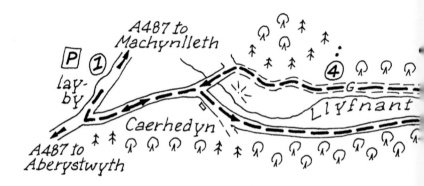

22

lane narrows to nothing, cross the stile on the LEFT, by the brick tank, and go through the gateposts to meet another lane, where you turn LEFT. Follow the lane, across an open field, to a clump of conifers, beyond which the route runs between a stone wall and a fence. Just beyond the end of the wall, take the RIGHT hand of two gates to enter the forest. The track forks immediately and you take the RIGHT hand, higher road. Carry on this road for ½ mile, slowly losing height and ignoring all side turns, through forest whichbecomes dense with rhododendrons, to such an extent that it seems almost tropical. *Where the river is visible, just below, look out for the adit on the far side and, a few yards further on, the dry trial adit, slightly up the bank on the right of the road.*

4 Soon you leave the forest by a gate and follow the track by the field fence, to pass a house on the right, with a spoil heap in the trees above. You soon reach a ruin on the left and then, in 200 yards, reach a road junction, where you turn LEFT to cross the river by a bridge and in a few yards join the lane, which takes you back to the main road and the starting point.

The Llyfnant Valley

Walk 13

PISTYLL Y LLYN & CWM RHAIADR FROM THE LLYFNANT VALLEY

DESCRIPTION A shorter walk of about 4½ miles with panoramic views of the northern hills, some awesome views into Cwm Rhaiadr and glimpses across the plateau to Pumlumon. You pass a high point of 1600 feet. The challenging descent via Llechwedd Melyn may be too daunting for inexperienced walkers and may not be suitable for those without a strong head for heights – if you have any doubts do not be ashamed to retrace your route to get home. *The near vertical face means that it must not be attempted in poor visibility or icy conditions.* Allow 2½ –3 hours.

START Junction by Cwmyrhaiadr farm at [SN 757963]

DIRECTIONS Of the A487, just north of Glandyfi at SN702974, take the minor road to the east and drive for 2 miles, bearing right at the first junction, along the delightful Llyfnant Valley to Glaspwll. Bear right in the hamlet at the junction and drive up the valley for 1½ miles, to park opposite the turn to Cwmyrhaiadr.

I Walk down the drive to Cwmyrhaiadr, over the river bridge and up to the farm buildings. A sign ahead points to the waterfall, but this is the return route. On the LEFT a slope doubles back in front of a large farm building and at the far end of the building a gate leads to an old track, which ascends the field to another gate. Through this gate the main track bears left, but you go ahead up a gully-like, sunken track, which is a little overgrown with gorse. Soon you pass the end of a grassy wall bank, which seems to be the continuation of wire fence from higher up the hillside, and vague wheel tracks cross right to left. The paths are rather confused here, but the right of way is a couple of degrees to the east of south and about 20 yards fur-

ther up the hill an old post comes into view ahead, to the left of a square fenced area around an old TV aerial post. From the post, the next fence can be seen, and you make for the gate. A further fence is now in view but a good deal of it has collapsed and the position of the gate is not evident. However, vague wheel tracks pass to the RIGHT of the longer length of standing wire , and these are heading in the correct direction. From this fence, the next fence is again in view, but the gate is hidden to your left by the ridge rising on that side. Take a line to top the ridge before the fence and the gate should be in front of you. Once through this gate you follow a more distinct path, which leads you up the ridge on your left, above the mountain road, which is now evident. Follow this path along the ridge for ½ mile, passing to the left of a small pool, and joining the mountain road just to the left of the stream which issues from a pipe into the large gully. *Views to the north have been widening all the way up the hillside and now views into Cwm Rhaiadr are stunning.*

2 Turn RIGHT onto the road and continue for about 350 yards to the first left hand hairpin. After the little bump on the right roadside and before the road is cut through a rocky area, step up the right bank and see the tops of conifers about 200 yards away and the summit of Plynlimon in the distance. Look for the vague path which lines up with Pumlumon and it should take you to a stile into the forest, where you follow the path down the ride to meet the forest road. Turn RIGHT and after 150 yards take the next forest ride on the RIGHT and follow a wet path through the trees to a stile out of the forest. Follow the path on for 300 yards, curving north-northwest, round the hillside, heading towards the cliffs just to the right of the stream which dives over the edge to form the waterfall of Pistyll y Llyn.

3 *Care is needed here*; this is Llechwedd Melyn. The narrow path descends to the RIGHT, across the steep slope, sheer at first, into the valley *and if you can take your eyes off the ground, the view is quite splendid.* After 600 yards you reach the second stand of pines, and the cliff is now behind.

4 *Your objective is the shaft of Cwmrhaiadr mine, which is in the small group of trees, with a rectangular fence, beyond the junction of the two gullies below.* The right of way takes you down the right side of the first gully, in a straight line to the mine, however it does not 'go' too well. Take good care as you pick a route across the stream to the mine. *This old mine, little more than a trial, has the remains of a wheel pit, still straddled by the cast iron hub of the old wheel, which has not turned in almost one hundred and fifty years. The open shaft is close to the wheel, guarded by the trees, and, below the rubbish-runs in the gully, a stream runs out of the collapsed adit. At the head of the valley is the high fall of Pistyll y Llyn.* Leaving the mine, follow the track roughly northwards for about a mile, past the iron shed and by stiles through a very wet plantation, by fields and gates to the buildings of Cwmyrhaiadr farm, where you then retrace your route back to the start.

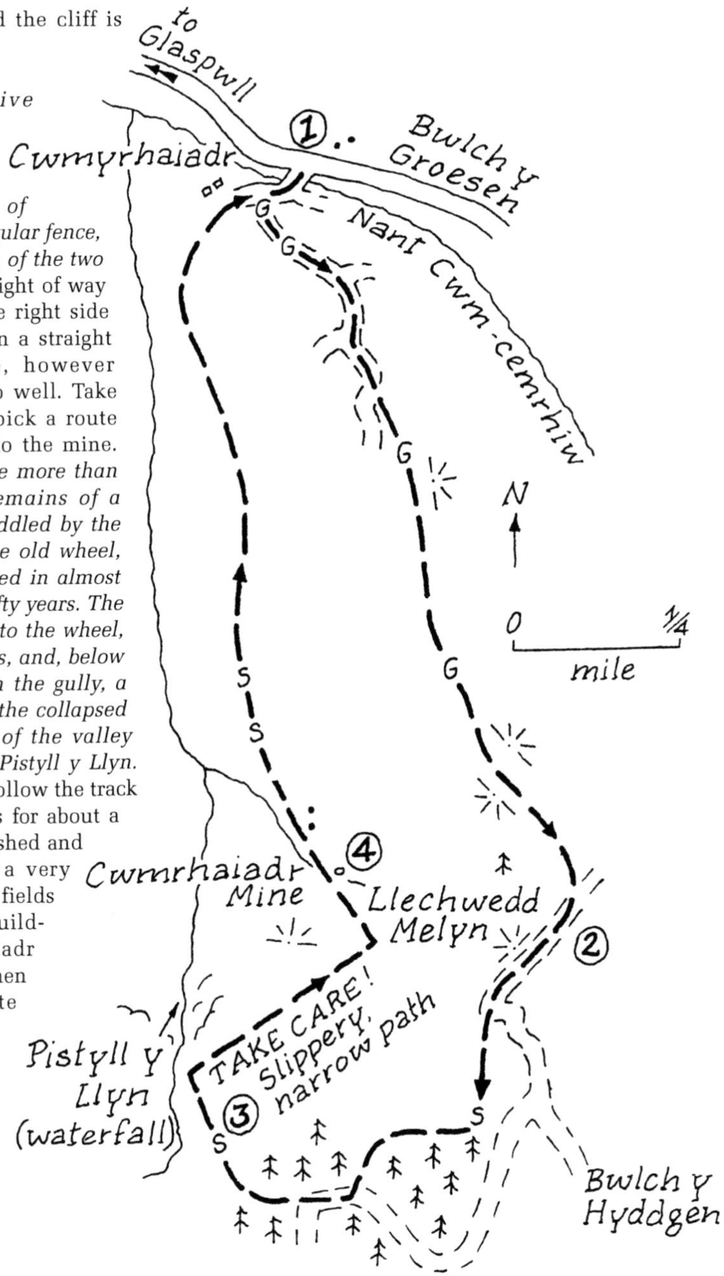

to Glaspwll

Cwmyrhaiadr

①

Bwlch y Groesen

Nant Cwm-cemrhiw

N

0 — ¼ mile

Cwmrhaiadr Mine ④

Llechwedd Melyn ②

✦

Pistyll y Llyn (waterfall)

③

TAKE CARE! Slippery, narrow path

S

Bwlch y Hyddgen

Walk 14

TALBONTDRAIN CIRCULAR

DESCRIPTION A walk of 8 miles, taking in two of the deep northern valleys. You climb through forest and cross part of the plateau on a mountain road to the high point of 1700 feet. There are fine views of Carn Hyddgen and Pumlumon from the climb, and the views of the northern peaks are also excellent. The descent is by grassy tracks and fields to end with a lovely riverside path in a forested valley. Allow 4½ hours.

START Lay-by on forest road beyond Talbontdrain [SN 778954]

DIRECTIONS To the east of Machynlleth centre, take the minor road on the right, by the ATS Tyre Centre, signed 'Llanidloes via Mountain Road', cross the golf course to Forge and turn right, before the bridge, to Uwch y Garreg. Ignore the left turn after 1¼ miles and continue for a similar distance to the Talbontdrain Hill Walking Centre, after a series of S-bends. Drive on for ¼ mile and, just inside the forest, park in the wide area on the right, at a crossroads.

1 Walk south, downhill, along the tarmac road, which soon becomes a forest road. Ignoring the right fork, bear LEFT, onto the lesser road by the stream. Keep on and, just before the road leaves the forest, cross a bridge and pass the gate to Hengwmcyfeiliog, then go through a gate and across a footbridge. The road, now a green track, wiggles across uneven ground, *with views on the left to the steep valley below Tarren Hengwm,* soon entering trees to climb southwards on a stony track, to the ridge of Esgair y Gog. Ignore the side roads on the climb *but look out for the strangely shaped rowan on the right. The tree has bent over to form an arch, with the top touching the ground. The side branches have then grown upwards to produce a many-stemmed tree.* Near the top of the ridge, join a road and curve round to the south-east, keeping to the main route.

2 The ground ahead becomes more open and, just before some small wire enclosures, the cycle route *Lôn Las Cymru* comes in from the right. Carry on for a few yards, with views of Cairn Gwilym on the summit of Carn Hyddgen, until you turn LEFT through a bridle gate, to take the RIGHT hand of the two roads, rising gently up Esgair y Ffordd. After 100 yards or so, take the bridleway, signed RIGHT and in a few yards, turn sharp LEFT, to climb gently for ¾ mile to rejoin the mountain road after a gate. The road leaves the forest and continues to climb for another ¼ mile, eventually levelling out with views of Pumlumon.

3 The road goes east to the lakes of Llyn Cwm-byr and Bugeilyn, however, the right of way leaves the road as a vague path to the RIGHT, about 700 yards from the last gate. After 200 yards the path turns LEFT and re-crosses the mountain road to become a well-used path, rising above the left of the road, heading due north. Follow the path through the heather to the crest *and take a last look back to the Pumlumon ridge and a glimpse of the waters of Llyn Cwm-byr, with the deeply eroded valley below the cliffs of Tarren Gesail to the north.* Pass through the gate on the ridge, *to views of Cadair Idris, Aran Fawddwy and the northern peaks.* Follow the track downhill, near to the fence, to another gate. As the ground levels out, cut across the plateau to the LEFT, along the line of the ridge, to meet the fence again.

4 Take the way-marked gate, in the RIGHT hand fence, a few yards before the next cross fence, and go downhill for a few yards to meet an eroded track, which descends LEFT to join a green road. Turn RIGHT and follow the road down to the next hairpin, where you take the older road straight ahead, across a gully, into a field and down the ridge to join the newer road again through a gate. Carry on to the farm of Rhiw Gam, through a gate, bear RIGHT and then LEFT round the first building, turn LEFT through the gate between this building and the next, then turn RIGHT and then LEFT around the end of the house and on a few yards to the tarmac road, which leaves the farm to take

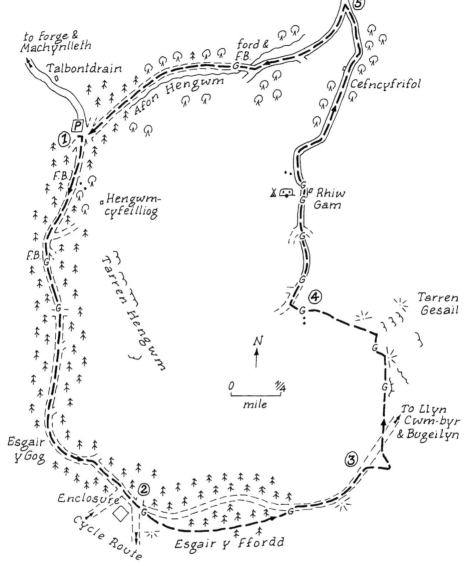

you onwards to Cefncyfrifol. Continue on the road from Cefncyfrifol for about ½ mile, before turning LEFT at the junction.

5 Follow the road left for just over ½ mile and, just before a bridge, turn RIGHT into the trees on a forest track. Drop down to a footbridge by a ford and, over the river, turn LEFT to a forest gate. The forest track runs for about a mile through a pleasant glen, by the river and, for those who still have the energy, a small stile on the left gives access to a waterfall in the gorge below. After nearly a mile you meet a larger forest road. Turn RIGHT and, after a few yards, turn LEFT to climb gently for about 50 yards to the cross-roads and the start of the walk.

Walk 15

WYNFORD VAUGHAN-THOMAS MONUMENT FROM ABERHOSAN

DESCRIPTION A walk of 6¼ miles around the last of the northern valleys which can be said to be 'West of Pumlumon'. You climb the ridge on a mountain road, join tarmac for a short way and then descend on mountain roads again. The views into the deep valleys are awe-inspiring and the Vaughan-Thomas Memorial viewpoint gives a panoramic vista of the northern peaks. Allow 3½ hours.

START Aberhosan [SN 809975]

DIRECTIONS To the east of Machynlleth centre, take the minor road on the right, by the ATS Tyre Centre, signed 'Llanidloes via Mountain Road', to the village of Forge. Continue over the bridge and through the village, and after about 3 miles turn right for Aberhosan along an even more minor road. After about a mile you reach the village and park whereever space permits. The car park down to the right now bears a sign banning parking.

I Walk uphill through the village, following the road for 600 yards to the farm of Ty-gwyn, where the tarmac gives way to stones. In another ½ mile, pass through a gate and the track becomes grassy. At the second gate, follow the track to put the fence on your RIGHT, do not be tempted by the right hand gate. Although it is at first a gentle climb up the ridge, as you reach the trees on our left, at the next gate, the pitch becomes quite steep and stony. *The larches at the edge of the forest seem rather prone to produce 'witches' brooms', more so than most of their kind in the area.*

2 At the top of the ridge, after ¾ mile of trees and several gates, leave the track through another gate to arrive at the viewpoint and memorial to Winford Vaughan-Thomas. It is worth a few minutes here to take in the views of the northern peaks. Leave the viewpoint and turn RIGHT up the tarmac road for nearly ½ mile, with a deep valley on your left, before turning RIGHT onto a mountain road, signed for 'Nature Reserve' and waymarked as *Glyndŵr's Way*. Carry on this road for about ½ mile, with the waters of Glaslyn ahead, and usually the odd bird watcher or fisherman.

3 Take the first turn RIGHT and somewhat backwards, following a bridleway sign, with a Glyndwr's Way waymark and, rising slightly, head towards the trig point on Foel Fadian. You soon swing LEFT, below the trig point, and pass close to the edge of the cliffs of Creigiau Eesgairfochnant, at the second marker post, to start the steep and wiggly descent of the ridge. *The deep valley of the Afon Dulas below is typical of the north-western valleys of the plateau, steep-sided and deeply eroded shale.* The track is over rock for a while and can be a little hard going; soon, however, you pass through a waymarked gate and the track becomes grassy, passing through several more way-marked gates. After about 1¼ miles, you pass the farm and caravan park of Esgair Fochnant, where the track becomes a lane and soon reaches the farm of Nantyfyda, where it swings RIGHT, around the buildings, to join a tarmac road.

4 The road soon swings LEFT and shortly take the right fork to the north. In just over ¼ mile Glyndŵr's Way branches off left, but keep to the tarmac road, to soon pass through the farm of Cefnwyr-grug, where the road wiggles around the buildings and continues north, until after ¼ mile it drops down into Aberhosan to return to the start.

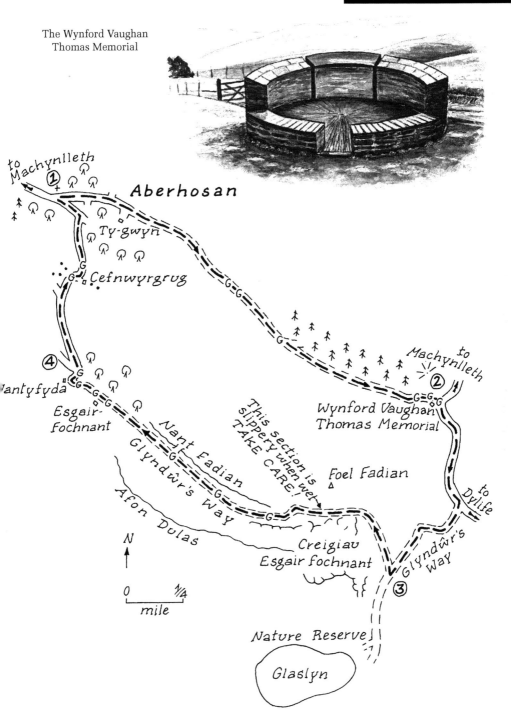

The Wynford Vaughan
Thomas Memorial

to Machynlleth

② + ⌢ ⌢
⌢ ⌢ ⌢

Aberhosan

Ty-gwyn

⌢ ⌢ ⌢

G Cefnwyrgrug

G-G

④

antyfyda
Esgair-fochnant

Nant Fadian

Glyndŵr's Way

This section is slippery when wet TAKE CARE!

to Machynlleth

②

G-G

Wynford Vaughan
Thomas Memorial

Foel Fadian
△

to Dylife

Afon Dulas

N
↑

Creigiau
Esgair Fochnant

Glyndŵr's Way

③

0   ¼
mile

Nature Reserve

Glaslyn

THE HAFAN INCLINE

DESCRIPTION A walk of almost 7 miles, initially following the route of an old narrow-gauge tramway and ascending the impressive 400 feet Hafan Incline to the high point of 1360 feet, with superb views of the lonely Cyneiniog valley. The way passes by a series of long-abandoned mine workings and offers views over the plateau, returning via a pleasant, winding forest road. Allow 4¼ hours.

START Bwlchglas Mine [SN 710877]

DIRECTIONS From Talybont village green [SN6558993] take the lane to the RIGHT of the Black Lion, bear right at the Victorian 'semis' and again right at the Y-junction, following the Bontgoch sign. Just under 2 miles from the village green, immediately after crossing a small stone bridge, take the left turn into a single-track gated lane and drive for about 1¾ miles until the valley opens out and the concrete remains or Bwlchglas mine appear on the right. There is space to park on the left.

*I*n the late 19th century it was decided to build a narrow-gauge tramway from the main line station at Llandre, through the village of Talybont, to the ridge of Cerig yr Hafan at the head of the Cyneiniog valley. The purpose being to transport the output of the recently opened quarry at Cerig yr Hafan and also at least four mines in the area, to the main line. By the time the tramway was operational some of the mines were already closed and the others on reducing production. The fortunes of the quarry fared no better and, although the stone was used to build Aberystwyth promenade, the quality of the stone was brought into question, leading to the early closure of the operation. The first sod for the tramway was cut in 1896 and the line closed in early 1899. Although traces of the tramway can be seen along much of the route, the most spectacular section is the Hafan Incline. This was a double-tracked inclined plane, 400ft in height at an angle of about 210, where loaded trucks were lowered

down one track on a cable, which passed round a large drum at the top, enabling the weight of the descending truck to haul up an empty truck on the other track.

I From the parking space, cross the road in front of the lower, flooded, Bwlchglas adit and take the path on the RIGHT of the workings, climbing diagonally right to soon reach a level path heading to the LEFT. This is the rail bed. *When the tramway was operational, Bwlchglas mine was temporarily closed, only to re-open in 1909, when the concrete foundations were installed.* Follow the rail bed through the mine buildings and up the valley, shortly diverting RIGHT to avoid a non-existent bridge. The track soon enters a patch of forestry via a cutting. Cross the stile above the cutting on the LEFT and follow the rather narrow track through the heather in the regenerating woodland, rising above the valley floor, for about ½ mile. *In at least two places small spoil heaps below the track show where veins of ore were cut and tried whilst building the rail bed.* Leave the woodland via a stile and continue for ½ mile or so to another non-existent bridge, just past a ruined cottage below. There are other tracks crossing the rail bed here; take the LEFT hand lower route. *The Hafan Incline is now in view at the head of the valley.* In another ½ mile into the narrowing valley the rail bed widens and the foot of the Incline is ahead. *The widened area allowed space for sidings and a runround loop. To your left in the gully are the spoil heaps of the Hafan mine lower adit, from which a stream flows down the gully. The stone structure ahead is the 1853 wheel pit for the Hafan mine, served by a leat, visible on the left hand hillside, which brought water 2¼ miles. Two small, vaulted adits are visible to the right of the incline.*

2 Pick your way across the water-eroded ground ahead and start the ascent of the Incline, driving yourself on with the prospect of the view from the top! *The incline is constructed over the north lode of the Hafan mine and in one place appears to have subsided into the workings. The south lode is to the right of the incline and is dangerous ground, with shafts, stopes and adits. **Best avoided.***

3 Pause for breath at the top and take in the view back down the Cyneiniog valley, then pick you way through the boulder-strewn area ahead to gain the gravel road in the quarry. *This quarry dates from 1956-61, the stone being used to build the Nant-y-moch dam, at the same time destroying the drum housing and upper works of the Incline.* Follow the road out of the quarry, passing another small, fenced quarry on the left, dropping down to a junction, with the small lake of Y Chwareli to the right, where you take the LEFT hand route to a gate. *Above, on the left, is a level track, the continuation of the tramway, which runs on to the original quarry in the forest. Below the tramway is a fenced shaft of Henfwlch mine.*

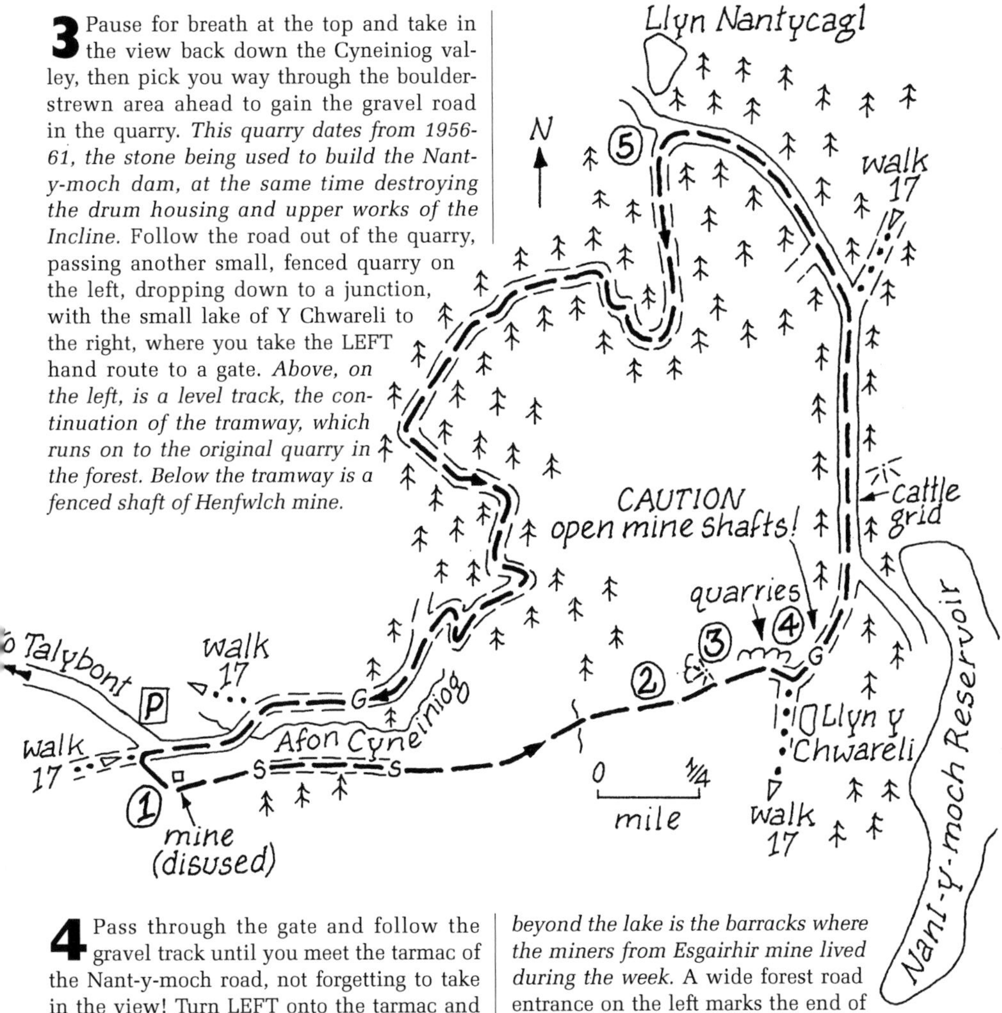

Llyn Nantycagl

N

⑤

walk 17

CAUTION open mine shafts!

cattle grid

quarries

③ ④

② G

Llyn y Chwareli

walk 17

Nant-y-moch Reservoir

o Talybont

walk 17

P

Afon Cyneiniog

walk 17

①

mine (disused)

0   ¼
mile

walk 17

4 Pass through the gate and follow the gravel track until you meet the tarmac of the Nant-y-moch road, not forgetting to take in the view! Turn LEFT onto the tarmac and continue for about 1¼ miles. *After a while, the forest on the right thins out and, after a cattle grid, looking back, Nant-y-moch reservoir comes into view, whilst across the valley the remains of Brynyrafr and Camdwrbach mines are visible, joined by part of Taylor's leat. Soon, the shaft of Eagle Brook mine appear on the right by the road, with an old shaft on the left, which makes a good lunch stop!* The road re-enters the trees and shortly passes a forest road on the LEFT. Keep to the tarmac. Climbing gently the trees eventually open out and Llyn Nantycagl comes into sight on the right. *The ruined building beyond the lake is the barracks where the miners from Esgairhir mine lived during the week.* A wide forest road entrance on the left marks the end of your route over tarmac.

5 Turn LEFT into the forest and follow the delightfully winding track for about 2½ miles, dropping back into the Cyneiniog valley, catching intriguing views of the surrounding hills through the trees on the way. Towards the end of the trees your outward route is visible on the hillside ahead. The track leaves the forest and passes through a gate, with your car now in sight, and winds round to the left to return to Bwlchglas mine.

31

OLD MINE ROAD TO ESGAIRHIR

DESCRIPTION A walk of 9½ miles, starting in the Cyneiniog valley and going by field tracks to reach the old mine road, which winds up a long, remote valley. You return via forest and mountain roads, having crossed the high point of 1440 feet. The views from the various vantage points are really worthwhile. The fords on route can be challenging after heavy rain. Allow 5½ hours.

START Bwlchglas Mine [SN 710877]

DIRECTIONS From Talybont village green take the lane to the RIGHT of the Black Lion, bear right at the Victorian semis and again right at the y-junction, following the Bont-goch sign. Just under 2 miles from the village green, immediately after crossing a small stone bridge, take the left turn into a single-track gated lane and drive for about 1¾ miles until the valley opens out and the concrete remains or Bwlchglas mine appear on the right. There is space to park on the left.

The current road from Talybont to Nant-y-moch reservoir is of fairly recent origin. The old miners' road, by which the workers made their weekly commute to the barracks at Esgairhir mine and by which the ore was carried to the smelters, took a much lonelier route. Ore was discovered at the site in 1689 and the mine worked off and on, until the final sale of equipment in 1902. A total of 7000 tons of lead ore were raised, over half before 1708.

I From the car, head up the valley, and follow the tarmac to cross the bridge over the Afon Cyneiniog. In a few yards, take the bridleway on the LEFT and keep on for ¼ mile to the ruins of Alltgochmyneydd farm. Pass round the buildings anti-clockwise, by the marker post, following the grassy track beyond the last building. A second marker post points through the bracken, down the field to a gate under the trees. Treat this gate with care, it opens away from you, to swing

over the waters of the ford beyond! This ford can be deep after rain. From the ford, the track climbs up a little and bears LEFT. Carry on up the track, keeping to the left of the low bank with trees, for 200 yards, until the bank and track turn RIGHT to a small wooden gate. Through the gate turn RIGHT and pass through three gates in front of a ruined building. Out of the last gate, turn LEFT and head diagonally up the field to a gate in the top fence. *Look back into the Cyneiniog valley for the view.*

2 Through the gate, turn RIGHT and stay by the fence, soon passing through a gate into the next field. In 200 yards, at the next gate, go through, turn LEFT and stick as close to the old stonewall on the left as the boggy ground will allow. Keep on, up this long, rising field for ½ mile, into the narrowing gap between the wall and the rocks on the right. *Views down to the left, into the Ceulan Valley, with the old workings of Blaen Ceulan mine across the modern Nant-y-moch road.* At the end of the field, you meet a stile in the corner, cross the stile and follow the faint wheel tracks for a few yards, into the dip, turning LEFT to cross the fence by another stile, just before the rising ground. About 75 yards from the stile, take the faint track to ascend the ridge to the RIGHT. Follow the edge of the ridge to meet a well-defined track coming up from the left. This is the old mine road.

3 Turn RIGHT to follow the mine road, *with views down to the infant Afon Cyneinog and the leat, which carried water 2½ miles to the Hafan mine.* Keep on the old road, wet in places, for ¾ mile, rising steadily to the head of the valley, after a long, right-handed dogleg. As you leave the valley, the way levels out and soon passes through a gate, with Pumlumon coming into view to the right. In 300 yards, you cross the tarmac Nant-y-moch road, dropping down to another ford, with Llyn Nantycagl on the right. Beyond the ford, the road climbs to the ruins of the Esgairhir barracks, passing through a gate to turn RIGHT behind the buildings. *This was home to the miners from Monday morning to Saturday evening, when they*

walked to the Black Lion Hotel in Talybont to collect their pay. Sundays were free to spend with family and chapel. Workings in the dip, to the left of the gate, date from 1690. The road winds round to the LEFT and, in ¼ mile, reaches a crossroads in an open, gravelled area.

4 Turn RIGHT along the broad road for 300 yards, to a forest gate. *To your left are the main workings of Esgairhir mine. CAUTION, there are open shafts here; if you must explore, do so with great care. The building housed a steam engine in the later years, the water power for this part of the workings came from a wheel ½ mile down the valley, beyond the route of the walk.* Through the gate, take the first forest road on the RIGHT and carry on for over a mile, part way

take the mountain road to the RIGHT, climbing for ¼ mile to pass through a gate.

5 Beyond the gate is a junction, ignore the side roads and go straight ahead. Keep on for 1 mile. Bear RIGHT and follow the road round towards the col on the ridge, ignoring the small track on the right by the yellow post. Climb the ½ mile to the col at Bwlch yr Adwy, passing through a gate halfway up. At the col, a track branches left, you keep RIGHT. Another mile of descent, with a gate halfway, leads

along passing through three bollards, descending gently at first but steeply, over a rocky surface, in the last 100 yards. At the end of the road is yet another ford, however a detour of a few strides through the trees on the LEFT brings you to a massive log bridge. Over the bridge and through more bollards, turn LEFT onto the tarmac. Carry on for ½ mile, passing by Eagle Brook mine, to a cattle grid. 100 yards past the cattle grid,

down the isolated valley to crest the ridge on the right hand side, above the Cyneiniog valley. When a stone wall and fence join you on your left, keep on for 75 yards and, just before the road passes through the wall, turn RIGHT onto a path and, after ¼ mile of descent, you will be back at the car.

Map labels:
④ ford
Llyn Nantycagl
walk 16
③
②
G-G
3 gates
G (ford)
Talybont
P ①
Afon Cyneiniog
walk 16
walk 16
cattle grid
⑤
Nant-y-Moch Reservoir
Llyn y Chwareli
Bwlch yr Adwy
walk 16
Alltgoch y mynydd
N
0   ¼
mile

THE SIX LAKES

DESCRIPTION A walk of 9 miles, visiting six different lakes, all of which are man-made in order to provide water power. Of the six lakes on the route, Llyn Nant-y-moch is the only one constructed in the 20th century and still used to produce power, being the main reservoir for the Rheidol Hydro-electric Scheme. All the other lakes were constructed in the mid 1800s to power water wheels at various mines. The route is mainly over mountain tracks, forest roads and grassy paths with many excellent views. The high point of 1300 feet is reached without any steep ascents. Allow 5½ hours.

START Car park at Llyn Pendam [SN 710839]

DIRECTIONS From the village of Penrhyncoch, bear right at the cross onto the Pont Erwyd road, leaving the local shop on the right. Carry on for about 4 miles, ignoring all side roads, as the road becomes a pleasant ridge route, at last twisting downhill with Llyn Pendam appearing on the right. Look out for the car park on the left.

1 From the car park turn RIGHT and walk a few yards along the tarmac towards the dam of Llyn Pendam. Take the diagonal path up the dam face for a few strides to the top, *with great views across the lake,* turn LEFT and follow the dam to an old sluice gate. *At this point a leat left Llyn Pendam to feed water to the next lake on our walk, Llyn Rhosgoch. Water also left Llyn Pendam at the far side to feed Cwmsymlog mine in the valley below.* Take the steep path down the dam face and follow the tarmac to the RIGHT for about ¼ mile, until Llyn Blaenmelindwr comes into view, and, as the road bends left, take the fisherman's stile on the RIGHT.

2 Follow the grassy path towards the bank ahead. *The leat from Llyn Rhosgoch to Bwlch mine is on the hillside to the left and on the right hand hillside is the incoming leat from Llyn Pendam.* Climb a few feet up the dam to the left of the sluice gate and the hidden lake of Llyn Rhosgoch is revealed. Turn LEFT along the dam to the end and then bear RIGHT to follow a faint track by the notice board, which heads to a low point in the ridge on the LEFT. Cross the ridge and cross a few yards of grass to the mountain road. Turn LEFT and follow the road towards Llyn Blaenmelindwr ahead, with the valley of Nant Cwm-y-graig on the right.

3 Leave the mountain road by the gate and turn RIGHT onto the tarmac for a few yards to the junction, where you turn LEFT, along the side of the lake and enter a forest area. After about ¼ mile the tarmac doubles back to the left but you take the forest road ahead, ignoring the higher, gated road, which soon appears on the right. Carry on the mountain road, ignoring a joining road on the left, and Llyn Syfrydin comes into view. Follow the shore of the lake, via a gate, to the far end, where you cross the small dam and sluice, which seems to pour the water into a bog. *Llyn Syfrydin was part of the Taylor's Leat system and supplied water to Goginan and Cwmbrwyno.*

4 Carry on, through another gate, along the mountain road, which bends LEFT in front of the old quarry, ignoring the track on the right. After about ¼ mile you reach a ford, just before a gate. Fortunately, a footbridge crosses the stream. Through the gate, turn RIGHT onto the narrower track, rising slowly, and follow this old, winding road for about ¾ mile. *This lonely road goes through several shallow cuttings in rocky outcrops, most of which show signs of wear from iron-tyred cartwheels. It was probably the road to Nant-y-moch farm, which was drowned when the lake of the same name was created.* After a steadily rising section, over a wet and water-worn surface, with much iron staining, take the RIGHT fork in the track into a more open area. Head towards the gate into the forest. Before the gate, it is worth a detour of a few yards to the LEFT, along the fence, to the higher ground, to take in the superb view over the western arm of Nant-y-moch.

5 Pass through the gate and follow the forest road for a little way to a junction, where you turn LEFT. Keep on this road, winding down through the trees, to the tarmac road at the edge of Llyn Nant-y-moch. Turn LEFT and follow the lake until the road doubles back around the far side. *The dry water course on the far bank is part of Taylor's leat system.* Cross the cattle grid and take the track almost immediately on the LEFT, soon passing through a gate. After about ¼ mile, turn RIGHT at the junction and in a few yards cross a ford – no footbridge this time.

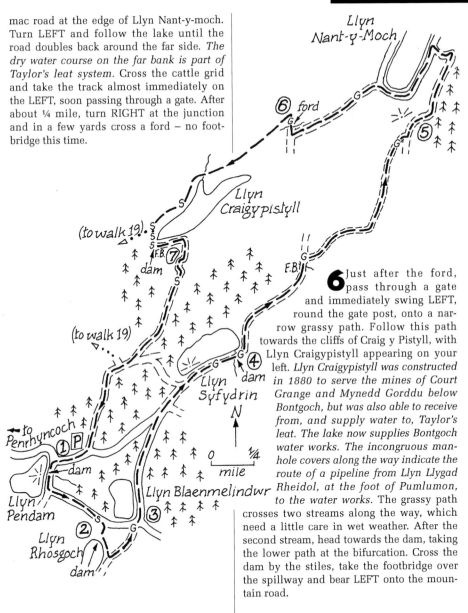

6 Just after the ford, pass through a gate and immediately swing LEFT, round the gate post, onto a narrow grassy path. Follow this path towards the cliffs of Craig y Pistyll, with Llyn Craigypistyll appearing on your left. *Llyn Craigypistyll was constructed in 1880 to serve the mines of Court Grange and Mynedd Gorddu below Bontgoch, but was also able to receive from, and supply water to, Taylor's leat. The lake now supplies Bontgoch water works. The incongruous manhole covers along the way indicate the route of a pipeline from Llyn Llygad Rheidol, at the foot of Pumlumon, to the water works.* The grassy path crosses two streams along the way, which need a little care in wet weather. After the second stream, head towards the dam, taking the lower path at the bifurcation. Cross the dam by the stiles, take the footbridge over the spillway and bear LEFT onto the mountain road.

7 Follow the road along the lakeside, soon turning RIGHT and heading uphill for 100 yards to cross a stile, by a gate, into the trees. Keep on for about 1 mile, ignoring the side turns, to reach the tarmac road, where you turn RIGHT and in a few yards reach the starting point.

WALK 19

THE UPPER LERI VALLEY

DESCRIPTION A walk of up to 5¾ miles, in the lonely valley, on the south bank of the Afon Leri, between the village of Bont-goch and the cliffs of Craig-Pistyll, returning by the north bank. The route is mainly over mountain roads and farm tracks, to a high point of 1200 feet, with contrasting prospects, up and down the valley. Allow 2½ hours.

START Road junction to the south of Bont-goch [SN 677856]

DIRECTIONS Approach Bont-goch from Talybont and the junction is through the village to the south. There is room for at least one car on the right-hand verge, behind the 'Bont-goch' sign.

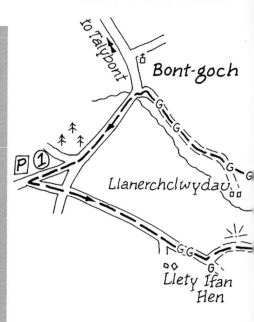

*I*n the 19th century the Afon Leri was a very important source of power for the industrial enterprises downstream. Water left the Leri at the top of the waterfall to feed Horridge's leat and just below the fall, water was tapped to serve Llawr-y-cwm-bach mine. Before the village, two more leats took water to Cwrt Grange and Mynyddgorddu mines. Below the village, the mines of Cefn Gwyn and Felin Fach used the water, whilst in Talybont the river powered the extensive mines and the tweed mills.

I From the car, take the lane on the LEFT beyond the signboard. Follow the lane, rising gently, for ½ mile, to a y-junction by Llety Ifan Hen farm. Take the LEFT, tarmaced fork and, in a few yards, pass through two gates in quick succession. Very soon, the track divides again, the right fork, with bridleway sign, passing through a gate. Turn LEFT before the gate and follow the mountain road, through a series of gates, for ½ mile. *Looking back, it is possible to pick out two leats crossing the marshy ground before the water works, whilst ahead you look down into the deepening Leri valley, with the cliffs of Craig-y-pistyll rising at the head.*

2 To the right of the track ahead is a rectangular conifer plantation, just beyond which is a gate on the track with a wooden bridle gate to the side. *The line of the Horridge leat, a forerunner of Taylor's leat, runs to the right from the base of the plantation.* Take the bridal gate. There is a choice of two routes here. For the shorter route, immediately take the less used track to the LEFT. In a few yards, the rough track bears right and a grassy path bears LEFT, heading diagonally down the hillside, towards a footbridge by the waste tips of Llawr-y-cwm-bach. You can take this path to cross the bridge and pass through two gates, to reach a track at the base of the tips (5), where you turn LEFT. For the longer route, carry on the original mountain road from the bridal gate for ¾ mile to enter the forest by a gate.

3 After few yards take the way-marked path on the LEFT, into the trees. Follow the path down through the larches, to reach an area of recent (2008) clear-cut. Cross the stream by the footbridge and carry on to the grassy area, beyond the clear-cut. Turn LEFT and head for the gap in the stone bank beyond the cottage and cross the Leri by the footbridge.

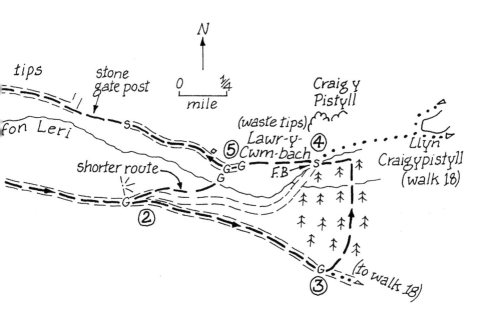

4 Keeping the strange gully on your right, head to the corner of the fence ahead. Keep between the base of the hill and the field fence, with the Llawr-y-cwm-bach leat above you on the right, and carry on to the mine tips. Follow the fence below the tips to meet the path from the footbridge. *The mine, like so many in the area, was worked in the second half of the 19th century, to little or no profit, recording only 470 tons of lead ore.*

5 From below the tips, the track heads for the farm, where you pass to the LEFT of the buildings, through the passage between the building and the fence. Keep on the track for about ¼ mile, through two old fence lines, to a gate with a way-marked stile to the left. Take the stile and, as the track loops round on the right, bear LEFT, to the isolated stone gate post in the centre of the field. Keep going to rejoin the track on the bank ahead and continue for another ¼ mile, passing the remains of Llanerchclwydau mine on your right – *not worked since the 17th century.* Pass through a gate and, as a farmhouse appears ahead, look out for a way-marked post on the right, turn RIGHT and, in a few yards pass through a gate into the field. Follow the line of trees to the far side of the field and turn RIGHT onto the track, through the way-marked gate. Keep on the track for ¼ mile, passing through a gate by a house on the left and then through another gate to the right of a large farm building. The track dog-legs LEFT, round a manure heap, and shortly reaches the main road, where you turn LEFT. Walk uphill out of the village to your car.

LLANDRE TO WALLOG & THE COAST PATH

DESCRIPTION A walk of 7 miles, from the village of Llandre, otherwise known as Llanfihangel-geneu'r-glyn, to the beach at Wallog, returning to Llandre via the Coast Path and Borth. The route uses country lanes, field tracks and part of the Ceredigion Coast Path. Despite the high point of only 540 feet, the views are still far-reaching and varied. The Coast Path section has a couple of steep ascents. Allow 4 hours.

START Lay-by on the B5435 in Llandre [SN 626872]

DIRECTIONS From the A487 in Bow Street, take the B4353, North West, towards Borth. After ¾ mile, just past a children's playground and a left turn to a level crossing, the lay-by is on the left by a phone box.

I From the car, head back towards Bow Street and take the first RIGHT over the level crossing. Continue up the road through the old part of the village but do not take the right turn below the church but, instead, at the top of the rise, bear RIGHT towards the lych gate. Just before the gate, turn LEFT up the steep gravel track with the black handrail. Follow the path, rising through the trees, for about 150 yards, to a junction by a wicket gate. Pass through the gate and in a few yards you come to a crossroads with a signpost. Turn the RIGHT. There is a gate ahead and one on your left. Take the LEFT-HAND gate and follow the track by the hedge on your right, soon passing through a gap in a hedge, which comes in from the left. Shortly a larger gap appears in the hedge, alongside an old shed, turn RIGHT through the gap and cross the field, keeping the hedge on your left, with the old sheds on the other side of the hedge, to reach a opening in the corner of the field. *The overgrown mound to your right is the site of Castell Gwallter, a fine example of a 'motte and bailey', dating from about 1110 and Anglo-Norman in origin.* Pass through

the opening, cross the small stream and follow the muddy track by the hedge to a stile onto the lane.

2 Over the stile, turn LEFT onto the tarmac and follow the lane for just over 1½ miles. The lane climbs gently to the high point of the walk, with distant views through the gaps in the hedges, before descending slowly through trees, to meet the larger road. Cross the larger road to enter the lane opposite, with the footpath sign. In a few yards, pass the first farm entrance on the right and shortly the lane itself bends right, into the farmyard. At the bend, take the green lane straight ahead, which, after an overgrown, muddy start, turns out to be an old cart road from the beach. Follow the lane for about ½ mile, until an elegant farm building appears on the right and a large house is ahead. Take the gate to the RIGHT of the house drive and head towards the beach, passing a small dam with a dilapidated sluice gate on the right. Follow the track onto the old sea wall.

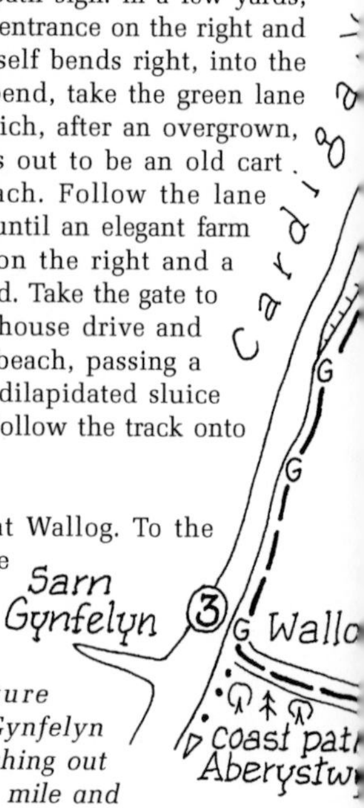

3 You are now at Wallog. To the south, on the grassy area is a large, disused *Sarn Gynfelyn* limekiln. *At low tide, the structure known as Sarn Gynfelyn can be seen, stretching out to sea for about ¼ mile and continuing under water for a further 6 miles. Legend has it that this is a causeway, built by Saint Cynfelyn, as a road to Ireland. Regardless of its origin, this rocky shelf was used as a landing site for ships carrying coal and limestone, which was carried by horse and cart up the causeway to the limekiln. The resulting lime was used as a fertilizer and for building.* Retrace your steps and turn LEFT across the dam, to follow the Coast Path northwards, for 1¾ miles, via stiles, gates and footbridges. The Coast Path passes quite close to the cliff edge in places, with considerable exposure. Although, going north, the ascents are steep, they do have a good footing, the descents, however,

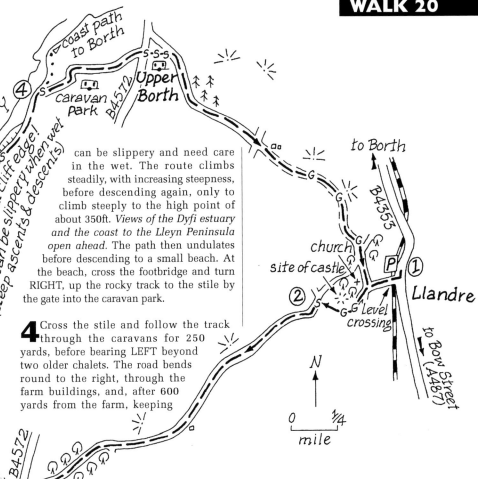

can be slippery and need care in the wet. The route climbs steadily, with increasing steepness, before descending again, only to climb steeply to the high point of about 350ft. *Views of the Dyfi estuary and the coast to the Lleyn Peninsula open ahead.* The path then undulates before descending to a small beach. At the beach, cross the footbridge and turn RIGHT, up the rocky track to the stile by the gate into the caravan park.

4 Cross the stile and follow the track through the caravans for 250 yards, before bearing LEFT beyond two older chalets. The road bends round to the right, through the farm buildings, and, after 600 yards from the farm, keeping

---

straight on, you reach the main road. Cross the road into the caravan park entrance opposite, with the footpath sign on the right-hand lamppost. Turn LEFT between the second and third caravans on your left – no signs. Pass between the third caravan and the fence, to a stile in the corner, cross this stile and two others in the next 100 yards, to meet a tarmac lane. Turn RIGHT. Follow the lane, climbing gently, for just over ½ mile, to a crossroads. Go straight ahead for about 100 yards, until the lane turns off into a farm on the left. Take the green lane straight ahead, climbing to a gate into a field. Keep to the

track by the left hand fence and pass through a second gate. *Views of the Dyfi estuary give way to views inland as height is gained.* The track descends to a third gate and soon joins tarmac at a hairpin bend, where you take the LEFT, lower road towards Llandre village. *Above, on your right, is the ancient graveyard and when you reach St Michael's church at the bottom of the slope, it is very worthwhile reading the information boards.* If energy permits explore the graveyard. Beyond the church, turn LEFT and retrace your steps to the level crossing and LEFT to the car.

A SHORT GLOSSARY OF MINING TERMS

Adit (Level) – Horizontal tunnel driven into the hillside to intersect the mineral vein.

Crusher – Heavy rollers which crushed the ore-bearing rock to facilitate the separation of waste.

Launder – A wooden trough carrying water: a mini aqueduct.

Leat – A man-made channel delivering water from a stream or pond to a waterwheel, often over long distances.

Open Cut – A trench in the ground where ore was worked from the surface.

Rubbish Run – Waste heaps where rock was tipped from small trucks running on rails.

Shaft – Vertical access from the surface to intersect adits underground.

Stope – The void left after ore has been removed, occasionally breaking through to the surface.

Tail Race – The channel carrying water away from a wheel.

Tramway – A narrow gauge railway for moving ore and waste, usually man-powered.

Wheel Pit – The housing for a waterwheel, often made of heavy masonry above ground.

KEY TO THE MAPS

- ➡ Walk route and direction
- ═ Metalled road
- ━ ━ Unsurfaced road
- •••• Footpath/route adjoining walk route
- ∿ River/stream
- ⚘ Trees
- ▰▰ Railway
- **G** Gate
- **S** Stile
- F.B. Footbridge
- ⩊ Viewpoint
- P Parking
- T Telephone
- ⛟ Caravan park

THE COUNTRY CODE

- Be safe – plan ahead and follow any signs
- Leave gates and property as you find them
- Protect plants and animals, and take your litter home
- Keep dogs under close control
- Consider other people

The CroW Act 2000, implemented throughout Wales in May 2005, introduced new legal rights of access for walkers to designated open country, predominantly mountain, moor, heath or down, plus all registered common land. This access can be subject to restrictions and closure for land management or safety reasons for up to 28 days a year.

Published by
Kittiwake 3 Glantwymyn Village Workshops, Glantwymyn, Machynlleth, Montgomeryshire SY20 8LY
© Text: Roger Handley 2010
© Maps & illustrations: Morag Perrott 2010

Cover pictures: Main – Llyn Nant y moch.
Inset – St Michael's church, Llandre. *David Perrott*

Printed by MWL, Pontypool.

First edition 2002. Reprinted 2005, 2009.
New enlarged edition 2010.
ISBN: 978 1 902302 78 2